The Life of King Henry V

Start Publishing PD LLC

Manufactured in the United States of America

Cover art: Shutterstock/Taisiya Kozorez

Cover design: Jennifer Do

10 9 8 7 6 5 4 3 2 1

ISBN 979-8-8809-1740-2

The Life of King Henry V

by William Shakespeare

DRAMATIS PERSONAE

CHORUS
KING HENRY THE FIFTH
DUKE OF GLOUCESTER, brother to the King
DUKE OF BEDFORD, brother to the King
DUKE OF EXETER, Uncle to the King
DUKE OF YORK, cousin to the King
EARL OF SALISBURY
EARL OF WESTMORELAND
EARL OF WARWICK
ARCHBISHOP OF CANTERBURY
BISHOP OF ELY
EARL OF CAMBRIDGE, conspirator against the King
LORD SCROOP, conspirator against the King
SIR THOMAS GREY, conspirator against the King
SIR THOMAS ERPINGHAM, officer in the King's army
GOWER, officer in the King's army
FLUELLEN, officer in the King's army
MACMORRIS, officer in the King's army
JAMY, officer in the King's army
BATES, soldier in the King's army
COURT, officer in the King's army
WILLIAMS, officer in the King's army
NYM, officer in the King's army
BARDOLPH, officer in the King's army
PISTOL, officer in the King's army
BOY A HERALD
CHARLES THE SIXTH, King of France
LEWIS, the Dauphin DUKE OF BURGUNDY
DUKE OF ORLEANS DUKE OF BRITAINE
DUKE OF BOURBON THE CONSTABLE OF FRANCE
RAMBURES, French Lord
GRANDPRE, French Lord
GOVERNOR OF HARFLEUR MONTJOY, a French herald
AMBASSADORS to the King of England
ISABEL, Queen of France
KATHERINE, daughter to Charles and Isabel
ALICE, a lady attending her

HOSTESS of the Boar's Head, Eastcheap; formerly Mrs. Quickly, now married to Pistol
Lords, Ladies, Officers, Soldiers, Messengers, Attendants

SCENE: *England and France*

PROLOGUE.

Enter Chorus

CHORUS: O for a Muse of fire, that would ascend
The brightest heaven of invention,
A kingdom for a stage, princes to act,
And monarchs to behold the swelling scene!
Then should the warlike Harry, like himself,
Assume the port of Mars; and at his heels,
Leash'd in like hounds, should famine, sword, and fire,
Crouch for employment. But pardon, gentles all,
The flat unraised spirits that hath dar'd
On this unworthy scaffold to bring forth
So great an object. Can this cockpit hold
The vasty fields of France? Or may we cram
Within this wooden O the very casques
That did affright the air at Agincourt?
O, pardon! since a crooked figure may
Attest in little place a million;
And let us, ciphers to this great accompt,
On your imaginary forces work.
Suppose within the girdle of these walls
Are now confin'd two mighty monarchies,
Whose high upreared and abutting fronts
The perilous narrow ocean parts asunder.
Piece out our imperfections with your thoughts:
Into a thousand parts divide one man,
And make imaginary puissance;
Think, when we talk of horses, that you see them
Printing their proud hoofs i' th' receiving earth;
For 'tis your thoughts that now must deck our kings,

Carry them here and there, jumping o'er times,
Turning th' accomplishment of many years
Into an hour-glass; for the which supply,
Admit me Chorus to this history;
Who prologue-like, your humble patience pray
Gently to hear, kindly to judge, our play.
Exit

ACT I. SCENE I. London. An Ante-Chamber in the King's Palace
Enter the Archbishop of Canterbury and the Bishop of Ely

CANTERBURY: My lord, I'll tell you: that self bill is urg'd
Which in th' eleventh year of the last king's reign
Was like, and had indeed against us pass'd
But that the scambling and unquiet time
Did push it out of farther question.

ELY: But how, my lord, shall we resist it now?

CANTERBURY: It must be thought on. If it pass against us,
We lose the better half of our possession;
For all the temporal lands which men devout
By testament have given to the church
Would they strip from us; being valu'd thus-
As much as would maintain, to the King's honour,
Full fifteen earls and fifteen hundred knights,
Six thousand and two hundred good esquires;
And, to relief of lazars and weak age,
Of indigent faint souls, past corporal toil,
A hundred alms-houses right well supplied;
And to the coffers of the King, beside,
A thousand pounds by th' year: thus runs the bill.

ELY: This would drink deep.

CANTERBURY: 'T would drink the cup and all.

ELY: But what prevention?

CANTERBURY: The King is full of grace and fair regard.

ELY: And a true lover of the holy Church.

CANTERBURY: The courses of his youth promis'd it not.
The breath no sooner left his father's body
But that his wildness, mortified in him,
Seem'd to die too; yea, at that very moment,
Consideration like an angel came
And whipp'd th' offending Adam out of him,
Leaving his body as a paradise
T'envelop and contain celestial spirits.
Never was such a sudden scholar made;
Never came reformation in a flood,
With such a heady currance, scouring faults;
Nor never Hydra-headed wilfulnes
So soon did lose his seat, and all at once,
As in this king.

ELY: We are blessed in the change.

CANTERBURY: Hear him but reason in divinity,
And, all-admiring, with an inward wish
You would desire the King were made a prelate;
Hear him debate of commonwealth affairs,
You would say it hath been all in all his study;
List his discourse of war, and you shall hear
A fearful battle rend'red you in music.
Turn him to any cause of policy,
The Gordian knot of it he will unloose,
Familiar as his garter; that, when he speaks,
The air, a charter'd libertine, is still,
And the mute wonder lurketh in men's ears
To steal his sweet and honey'd sentences;
So that the art and practic part of life

Must be the mistress to this theoric;
Which is a wonder how his Grace should glean it,
Since his addiction was to courses vain,
His companies unletter'd, rude, and shallow,
His hours fill'd up with riots, banquets, sports;
And never noted in him any study,
Any retirement, any sequestration
From open haunts and popularity.

ELY: The strawberry grows underneath the nettle,
And wholesome berries thrive and ripen best
Neighbour'd by fruit of baser quality;
And so the Prince obscur'd his contemplation
Under the veil of wildness; which, no doubt,
Grew like the summer grass, fastest by night,
Unseen, yet crescive in his faculty.

CANTERBURY: It must be so; for miracles are ceas'd;
And therefore we must needs admit the means
How things are perfected.

ELY: But, my good lord,
How now for mitigation of this bill
Urg'd by the Commons? Doth his Majesty
Incline to it, or no?

CANTERBURY: He seems indifferent
Or rather swaying more upon our part
Than cherishing th' exhibiters against us;
For I have made an offer to his Majesty-
Upon our spiritual convocation
And in regard of causes now in hand,
Which I have open'd to his Grace at large,
As touching France- to give a greater sum
Than ever at one time the clergy yet
Did to his predecessors part withal.

ELY: How did this offer seem receiv'd, my lord?

CANTERBURY: With good acceptance of his Majesty;
Save that there was not time enough to hear,
As I perceiv'd his Grace would fain have done,
The severals and unhidden passages
Of his true tides to some certain dukedoms,
And generally to the crown and seat of France,
Deriv'd from Edward, his great-grandfather.

ELY: What was th' impediment that broke this off?

CANTERBURY: The French ambassador upon that instant
Crav'd audience; and the hour, I think, is come
To give him hearing: is it four o'clock?

ELY: It is.

CANTERBURY: Then go we in, to know his embassy;
Which I could with a ready guess declare,
Before the Frenchman speak a word of it.

ELY: I'll wait upon you, and I long to hear it.
Exeunt

ACT I. SCENE II. London. The Presence Chamber in the King's palace

Enter the King, Gloucester, Bedford, Exeter, Warwick, Westmoreland, and Attendants

KING HENRY: Where is my gracious Lord of Canterbury?

EXETER: Not here in presence.

KING HENRY: Send for him, good uncle.

WESTMORELAND: Shall we call in th' ambassador, my liege?

KING HENRY: Not yet, my cousin; we would be resolv'd,
Before we hear him, of some things of weight
That task our thoughts, concerning us and France.

Enter the Archbishop of Canterbury and the Bishop of Ely

CANTERBURY: God and his angels guard your sacred throne,
And make you long become it!

KING HENRY: Sure, we thank you.
My learned lord, we pray you to proceed,
And justly and religiously unfold
Why the law Salique, that they have in France,
Or should or should not bar us in our claim;
And God forbid, my dear and faithful lord,
That you should fashion, wrest, or bow your reading,
Or nicely charge your understanding soul
With opening titles miscreate whose right
Suits not in native colours with the truth;
For God doth know how many, now in health,
Shall drop their blood in approbation
Of what your reverence shall incite us to.
Therefore take heed how you impawn our person,
How you awake our sleeping sword of war-
We charge you, in the name of God, take heed;
For never two such kingdoms did contend
Without much fall of blood; whose guiltless drops
Are every one a woe, a sore complaint,
'Gainst him whose wrongs gives edge unto the swords
That makes such waste in brief mortality.
Under this conjuration speak, my lord;
For we will hear, note, and believe in heart,
That what you speak is in your conscience wash'd
As pure as sin with baptism.

CANTERBURY: Then hear me, gracious sovereign, and you peers,
That owe yourselves, your lives, and services,

To this imperial throne. There is no bar
To make against your Highness' claim to France
But this, which they produce from Pharamond:
'In terram Salicam mulieres ne succedant'-
'No woman shall succeed in Salique land';
Which Salique land the French unjustly gloze
To be the realm of France, and Pharamond
The founder of this law and female bar.
Yet their own authors faithfully affirm
That the land Salique is in Germany,
Between the floods of Sala and of Elbe;
Where Charles the Great, having subdu'd the Saxons,
There left behind and settled certain French;
Who, holding in disdain the German women
For some dishonest manners of their life,
Establish'd then this law: to wit, no female
Should be inheritrix in Salique land;
Which Salique, as I said, 'twixt Elbe and Sala,
Is at this day in Germany call'd Meisen.
Then doth it well appear the Salique law
Was not devised for the realm of France;
Nor did the French possess the Salique land
Until four hundred one and twenty years
After defunction of King Pharamond,
Idly suppos'd the founder of this law;
Who died within the year of our redemption
Four hundred twenty-six; and Charles the Great
Subdu'd the Saxons, and did seat the French
Beyond the river Sala, in the year
Eight hundred five. Besides, their writers say,
King Pepin, which deposed Childeric,
Did, as heir general, being descended
Of Blithild, which was daughter to King Clothair,
Make claim and title to the crown of France.
Hugh Capet also, who usurp'd the crown
Of Charles the Duke of Lorraine, sole heir male
Of the true line and stock of Charles the Great,

To find his title with some shows of truth-
Though in pure truth it was corrupt and naught-
Convey'd himself as th' heir to th' Lady Lingare,
Daughter to Charlemain, who was the son
To Lewis the Emperor, and Lewis the son
Of Charles the Great. Also King Lewis the Tenth,
Who was sole heir to the usurper Capet,
Could not keep quiet in his conscience,
Wearing the crown of France, till satisfied
That fair Queen Isabel, his grandmother,
Was lineal of the Lady Ermengare,
Daughter to Charles the foresaid Duke of Lorraine;
By the which marriage the line of Charles the Great
Was re-united to the Crown of France.
So that, as clear as is the summer's sun,
King Pepin's title, and Hugh Capet's claim,
King Lewis his satisfaction, all appear
To hold in right and tide of the female;
So do the kings of France unto this day,
Howbeit they would hold up this Salique law
To bar your Highness claiming from the female;
And rather choose to hide them in a net
Than amply to imbar their crooked tides
Usurp'd from you and your progenitors.

KING HENRY: May I with right and conscience make this claim?

CANTERBURY: The sin upon my head, dread sovereign!
For in the book of Numbers is it writ,
When the man dies, let the inheritance
Descend unto the daughter. Gracious lord,
Stand for your own, unwind your bloody flag,
Look back into your mighty ancestors.
Go, my dread lord, to your great-grandsire's tomb,
From whom you claim; invoke his warlike spirit,
And your great-uncle's, Edward the Black Prince,
Who on the French ground play'd a tragedy,

Making defeat on the fun power of France,
Whiles his most mighty father on a hill
Stood smiling to behold his lion's whelp
Forage in blood of French nobility.
O noble English, that could entertain
With half their forces the full pride of France,
And let another half stand laughing by,
All out of work and cold for action!

ELY: Awake remembrance of these valiant dead,
And with your puissant arm renew their feats.
You are their heir; you sit upon their throne;
The blood and courage that renowned them
Runs in your veins; and my thrice-puissant liege
Is in the very May-morn of his youth,
Ripe for exploits and mighty enterprises.

EXETER: Your brother kings and monarchs of the earth
Do all expect that you should rouse yourself,
As did the former lions of your blood.

WESTMORELAND: They know your Grace hath cause and means and might-
So hath your Highness; never King of England
Had nobles richer and more loyal subjects,
Whose hearts have left their bodies here in England
And lie pavilion'd in the fields of France.

CANTERBURY: O, let their bodies follow, my dear liege,
With blood and sword and fire to win your right!
In aid whereof we of the spiritualty
Will raise your Highness such a mighty sum
As never did the clergy at one time
Bring in to any of your ancestors.

KING HENRY: We must not only arm t' invade the French,
But lay down our proportions to defend
Against the Scot, who will make road upon us

With all advantages.

CANTERBURY: They of those marches, gracious sovereign,
Shall be a wall sufficient to defend
Our inland from the pilfering borderers.

KING HENRY: We do not mean the coursing snatchers only,
But fear the main intendment of the Scot,
Who hath been still a giddy neighbour to us;
For you shall read that my great-grandfather
Never went with his forces into France
But that the Scot on his unfurnish'd kingdom
Came pouring, like the tide into a breach,
With ample and brim fulness of his force,
Galling the gleaned land with hot assays,
Girdling with grievous siege castles and towns;
That England, being empty of defence,
Hath shook and trembled at th' ill neighbourhood.

CANTERBURY: She hath been then more fear'd than harm'd, my liege;
For hear her but exampled by herself:
When all her chivalry hath been in France,
And she a mourning widow of her nobles,
She hath herself not only well defended
But taken and impounded as a stray
The King of Scots; whom she did send to France,
To fill King Edward's fame with prisoner kings,
And make her chronicle as rich with praise
As is the ooze and bottom of the sea
With sunken wreck and sumless treasuries.

WESTMORELAND: But there's a saying, very old and true:
'If that you will France win,
Then with Scotland first begin.'
For once the eagle England being in prey,
To her unguarded nest the weasel Scot
Comes sneaking, and so sucks her princely eggs,

Playing the mouse in absence of the cat,
To tear and havoc more than she can eat.

EXETER: It follows, then, the cat must stay at home;
Yet that is but a crush'd necessity,
Since we have locks to safeguard necessaries
And pretty traps to catch the petty thieves.
While that the armed hand doth fight abroad,
Th' advised head defends itself at home;
For government, though high, and low, and lower,
Put into parts, doth keep in one consent,
Congreeing in a full and natural close,
Like music.

CANTERBURY: Therefore doth heaven divide
The state of man in divers functions,
Setting endeavour in continual motion;
To which is fixed as an aim or but
Obedience; for so work the honey bees,
Creatures that by a rule in nature teach
The act of order to a peopled kingdom.
They have a king, and officers of sorts,
Where some like magistrates correct at home;
Others like merchants venture trade abroad;
Others like soldiers, armed in their stings,
Make boot upon the summer's velvet buds,
Which pillage they with merry march bring home
To the tent-royal of their emperor;
Who, busied in his majesty, surveys
The singing masons building roofs of gold,
The civil citizens kneading up the honey,
The poor mechanic porters crowding in
Their heavy burdens at his narrow gate,
The sad-ey'd justice, with his surly hum,
Delivering o'er to executors pale
The lazy yawning drone. I this infer,
That many things, having full reference

To one consent, may work contrariously;
As many arrows loosed several ways
Come to one mark, as many ways meet in one town,
As many fresh streams meet in one salt sea,
As many lines close in the dial's centre;
So many a thousand actions, once afoot,
End in one purpose, and be all well home
Without defeat. Therefore to France, my liege.
Divide your happy England into four;
Whereof take you one quarter into France,
And you withal shall make all Gallia shake.
If we, with thrice such powers left at home,
Cannot defend our own doors from the dog,
Let us be worried, and our nation lose
The name of hardiness and policy.

KING HENRY: Call in the messengers sent from the Dauphin.
Exeunt Some Attendants
Now are we well resolv'd; and, by God's help
And yours, the noble sinews of our power,
France being ours, we'll bend it to our awe,
Or break it all to pieces; or there we'll sit,
Ruling in large and ample empery
O'er France and all her almost kingly dukedoms,
Or lay these bones in an unworthy urn,
Tombless, with no remembrance over them.
Either our history shall with full mouth
Speak freely of our acts, or else our grave,
Like Turkish mute, shall have a tongueless mouth,
Not worshipp'd with a waxen epitaph.
Enter Ambassadors of France
Now are we well prepar'd to know the pleasure
Of our fair cousin Dauphin; for we hear
Your greeting is from him, not from the King.

AMBASSADOR: May't please your Majesty to give us leave
Freely to render what we have in charge;

Or shall we sparingly show you far of
The Dauphin's meaning and our embassy?

KING HENRY: We are no tyrant, but a Christian king,
Unto whose grace our passion is as subject
As are our wretches fett'red in our prisons;
Therefore with frank and with uncurbed plainness
Tell us the Dauphin's mind.

AMBASSADOR: Thus then, in few.
Your Highness, lately sending into France,
Did claim some certain dukedoms in the right
Of your great predecessor, King Edward the Third.
In answer of which claim, the Prince our master
Says that you savour too much of your youth,
And bids you be advis'd there's nought in France
That can be with a nimble galliard won;
You cannot revel into dukedoms there.
He therefore sends you, meeter for your spirit,
This tun of treasure; and, in lieu of this,
Desires you let the dukedoms that you claim
Hear no more of you. This the Dauphin speaks.

KING HENRY: What treasure, uncle?

EXETER: Tennis-balls, my liege.

KING HENRY: We are glad the Dauphin is so pleasant with us;
His present and your pains we thank you for.
When we have match'd our rackets to these balls,
We will in France, by God's grace, play a set
Shall strike his father's crown into the hazard.
Tell him he hath made a match with such a wrangler
That all the courts of France will be disturb'd
With chaces. And we understand him well,
How he comes o'er us with our wilder days,
Not measuring what use we made of them.

We never valu'd this poor seat of England;
And therefore, living hence, did give ourself
To barbarous licence; as 'tis ever common
That men are merriest when they are from home.
But tell the Dauphin I will keep my state,
Be like a king, and show my sail of greatness,
When I do rouse me in my throne of France;
For that I have laid by my majesty
And plodded like a man for working-days;
But I will rise there with so full a glory
That I will dazzle all the eyes of France,
Yea, strike the Dauphin blind to look on us.
And tell the pleasant Prince this mock of his
Hath turn'd his balls to gun-stones, and his soul
Shall stand sore charged for the wasteful vengeance
That shall fly with them; for many a thousand widows
Shall this his mock mock of their dear husbands;
Mock mothers from their sons, mock castles down;
And some are yet ungotten and unborn
That shall have cause to curse the Dauphin's scorn.
But this lies all within the will of God,
To whom I do appeal; and in whose name,
Tell you the Dauphin, I am coming on,
To venge me as I may and to put forth
My rightful hand in a well-hallow'd cause.
So get you hence in peace; and tell the Dauphin
His jest will savour but of shallow wit,
When thousands weep more than did laugh at it.
Convey them with safe conduct. Fare you well.
Exeunt Ambassadors

EXETER: This was a merry message.

KING HENRY: We hope to make the sender blush at it.
Therefore, my lords, omit no happy hour
That may give furth'rance to our expedition;
For we have now no thought in us but France,

Save those to God, that run before our business.
Therefore let our proportions for these wars
Be soon collected, and all things thought upon
That may with reasonable swiftness ad
More feathers to our wings; for, God before,
We'll chide this Dauphin at his father's door.
Therefore let every man now task his thought
That this fair action may on foot be brought.
Exeunt

ACT II. PROLOGUE. Flourish. Enter Chorus

CHORUS: Now all the youth of England are on fire,
And silken dalliance in the wardrobe lies;
Now thrive the armourers, and honour's thought
Reigns solely in the breast of every man;
They sell the pasture now to buy the horse,
Following the mirror of all Christian kings
With winged heels, as English Mercuries.
For now sits Expectation in the air,
And hides a sword from hilts unto the point
With crowns imperial, crowns, and coronets,
Promis'd to Harry and his followers.
The French, advis'd by good intelligence
Of this most dreadful preparation,
Shake in their fear and with pale policy
Seek to divert the English purposes.
O England! model to thy inward greatness,
Like little body with a mighty heart,
What mightst thou do that honour would thee do,
Were all thy children kind and natural!
But see thy fault! France hath in thee found out
A nest of hollow bosoms, which he fills
With treacherous crowns; and three corrupted men-
One, Richard Earl of Cambridge, and the second,
Henry Lord Scroop of Masham, and the third,
Sir Thomas Grey, knight, of Northumberland,

Have, for the gilt of France- O guilt indeed!-
Confirm'd conspiracy with fearful France;
And by their hands this grace of kings must die-
If hell and treason hold their promises,
Ere he take ship for France- and in Southampton.
Linger your patience on, and we'll digest
Th' abuse of distance, force a play.
The sum is paid, the traitors are agreed,
The King is set from London, and the scene
Is now transported, gentles, to Southampton;
There is the play-house now, there must you sit,
And thence to France shall we convey you safe
And bring you back, charming the narrow seas
To give you gentle pass; for, if we may,
We'll not offend one stomach with our play.
But, till the King come forth, and not till then,
Unto Southampton do we shift our scene.
Exit

ACT II. SCENE I. London. Before the Boar's Head Tavern, Eastcheap
Enter Corporal Nym and Lieutenant Bardolph

BARDOLPH: Well met, Corporal Nym.

NYM: Good morrow, Lieutenant Bardolph.

BARDOLPH: What, are Ancient Pistol and you friends yet?

NYM: For my part, I care not; I say little, but when time shall serve, there shall be smiles- but that shall be as it may. I dare not fight; but I will wink and hold out mine iron. It is a simple one; but what though? It will toast cheese, and it will endure cold as another man's sword will; and there's an end.

BARDOLPH: I will bestow a breakfast to make you friends; and we'll be all three sworn brothers to France. Let't be so, good Corporal Nym.

NYM: Faith, I will live so long as I may, that's the certain of it; and when I cannot live any longer, I will do as I may. That is my rest, that is the rendezvous of it.

BARDOLPH: It is certain, Corporal, that he is married to Nell Quickly; and certainly she did you wrong, for you were troth-plight to her.

NYM: I cannot tell; things must be as they may. Men may sleep, and they may have their throats about them at that time; and some say knives have edges. It must be as it may; though patience be a tired mare, yet she will plod. There must be conclusions. Well, I cannot tell.

Enter Pistol and Hostess

BARDOLPH: Here comes Ancient Pistol and his wife. Good Corporal, be patient here.

NYM: How now, mine host Pistol!

PISTOL: Base tike, call'st thou me host?
Now by this hand, I swear I scorn the term;
Nor shall my Nell keep lodgers.

HOSTESS: No, by my troth, not long; for we cannot lodge and board a dozen or fourteen gentlewomen that live honestly by the prick of their needles, but it will be thought we keep a bawdy-house straight. *Nym Draws* O well-a-day, Lady, if he be not drawn! Now we shall see wilful adultery and murder committed.

BARDOLPH: Good Lieutenant, good Corporal, offer nothing here.

NYM: Pish!

PISTOL: Pish for thee, Iceland dog! thou prick-ear'd cur of Iceland!

HOSTESS: Good Corporal Nym, show thy valour, and put up your sword.

NYM: Will you shog off? I would have you solus.

PISTOL: 'Solus,' egregious dog? O viper vile!
The 'solus' in thy most mervailous face;
The 'solus' in thy teeth, and in thy throat,
And in thy hateful lungs, yea, in thy maw, perdy;
And, which is worse, within thy nasty mouth!
I do retort the 'solus' in thy bowels;
For I can take, and Pistol's cock is up,
And flashing fire will follow.

NYM: I am not Barbason: you cannot conjure me. I have an humour to knock you indifferently well. If you grow foul with me, Pistol, I will scour you with my rapier, as I may, in fair terms; if you would walk off I would prick your guts a little, in good terms, as I may, and thaes the humour of it.

PISTOL: O braggart vile and damned furious wight!
The grave doth gape and doting death is near;
Therefore exhale. *Pistol Draws*

BARDOLPH: Hear me, hear me what I say: he that strikes the first stroke I'll run him up to the hilts, as I am a soldier. *Draws*

PISTOL: An oath of mickle might; and fury shall abate.
Pistol and Nym Sheathe Their Swords
Give me thy fist, thy fore-foot to me give;
Thy spirits are most tall.

NYM: I will cut thy throat one time or other, in fair terms; that is the humour of it.

PISTOL: 'Couple a gorge!'
That is the word. I thee defy again.
O hound of Crete, think'st thou my spouse to get?
No; to the spital go,
And from the powd'ring tub of infamy
Fetch forth the lazar kite of Cressid's kind,
Doll Tearsheet she by name, and her espouse.
I have, and I will hold, the quondam Quickly

For the only she; and- pauca, there's enough.
Go to.
Enter the Boy

BOY: Mine host Pistol, you must come to my master; and your hostess- he is very sick, and would to bed. Good Bardolph, put thy face between his sheets, and do the office of a warming-pan. Faith, he's very ill.

BARDOLPH: Away, you rogue.

HOSTESS: By my troth, he'll yield the crow a pudding one of these days: the King has kill'd his heart. Good husband, come home presently.
Exeunt Hostess and Boy

BARDOLPH: Come, shall I make you two friends? We must to France together; why the devil should we keep knives to cut one another's throats?

PISTOL: Let floods o'erswell, and fiends for food howl on!

NYM: You'll pay me the eight shillings I won of you at betting?

PISTOL: Base is the slave that pays.

NYM: That now I will have; that's the humour of it.

PISTOL: As manhood shall compound: push home.
Pistol and Nym Draw

BARDOLPH: By this sword, he that makes the first thrust I'll kill him; by this sword, I will.

PISTOL: Sword is an oath, and oaths must have their course.
Sheathes His Sword

BARDOLPH: Corporal Nym, an thou wilt be friends, be friends; an thou wilt not, why then be enemies with me too. Prithee put up.

NYM: I shall have my eight shillings I won of you at betting?

PISTOL: A noble shalt thou have, and present pay;
And liquor likewise will I give to thee,
And friendship shall combine, and brotherhood.
I'll live by Nym and Nym shall live by me.
Is not this just? For I shall sutler be
Unto the camp, and profits will accrue.
Give me thy hand.

NYM: *Sheathing His Sword* I shall have my noble?

PISTOL: In cash most justly paid.

NYM: *Shaking hands* Well, then, that's the humour of't.
Re-enter Hostess

HOSTESS: As ever you come of women, come in quickly to Sir John. Ah, poor heart! he is so shak'd of a burning quotidian tertian that it is most lamentable to behold. Sweet men, come to him.

NYM: The King hath run bad humours on the knight; that's the even of it.

PISTOL: Nym, thou hast spoke the right;
His heart is fracted and corroborate.

NYM: The King is a good king, but it must be as it may; he passes some humours and careers.

PISTOL: Let us condole the knight; for, lambkins, we will live.
Exeunt

ACT II. SCENE II. Southampton. A Council-Chamber

Enter Exeter, Bedford, and Westmoreland

BEDFORD: Fore God, his Grace is bold, to trust these traitors.

EXETER: They shall be apprehended by and by.

WESTMORELAND: How smooth and even they do bear themselves,
As if allegiance in their bosoms sat,
Crowned with faith and constant loyalty!

BEDFORD: The King hath note of all that they intend,
By interception which they dream not of.

EXETER: Nay, but the man that was his bedfellow,
Whom he hath dull'd and cloy'd with gracious favours-
That he should, for a foreign purse, so sell
His sovereign's life to death and treachery!
Trumpets Sound. Enter the King, Scroop, Cambridge, Grey, and Attendants

KING HENRY: Now sits the wind fair, and we will aboard.
My Lord of Cambridge, and my kind Lord of Masham,
And you, my gentle knight, give me your thoughts.
Think you not that the pow'rs we bear with us
Will cut their passage through the force of France,
Doing the execution and the act
For which we have in head assembled them?

SCROOP: No doubt, my liege, if each man do his best.

KING HENRY: I doubt not that, since we are well persuaded
We carry not a heart with us from hence
That grows not in a fair consent with ours;
Nor leave not one behind that doth not wish
Success and conquest to attend on us.

CAMBRIDGE: Never was monarch better fear'd and lov'd
Than is your Majesty. There's not, I think, a subject
That sits in heart-grief and uneasines
Under the sweet shade of your government.

GREY: True: those that were your father's enemies

Have steep'd their galls in honey, and do serve you
With hearts create of duty and of zeal.

KING HENRY: We therefore have great cause of thankfulness,
And shall forget the office of our hand
Sooner than quittance of desert and merit
According to the weight and worthiness.

SCROOP: So service shall with steeled sinews toil,
And labour shall refresh itself with hope,
To do your Grace incessant services.

KING HENRY: We judge no less. Uncle of Exeter,
Enlarge the man committed yesterday
That rail'd against our person. We consider
It was excess of wine that set him on;
And on his more advice we pardon him.

SCROOP: That's mercy, but too much security.
Let him be punish'd, sovereign, lest example
Breed, by his sufferance, more of such a kind.

KING HENRY: O, let us yet be merciful!

CAMBRIDGE: So may your Highness, and yet punish too.

GREY: Sir, You show great mercy if you give him life,
After the taste of much correction.

KING HENRY: Alas, your too much love and care of me
Are heavy orisons 'gainst this poor wretch!
If little faults proceeding on distemper
Shall not be wink'd at, how shall we stretch our eye
When capital crimes, chew'd, swallow'd, and digested,
Appear before us? We'll yet enlarge that man,
Though Cambridge, Scroop, and Grey, in their dear care
And tender preservation of our person,

Would have him punish'd. And now to our French causes:
Who are the late commissioners?

CAMBRIDGE: I one, my lord.
Your Highness bade me ask for it to-day.

SCROOP: So did you me, my liege.

GREY: And I, my royal sovereign.

KING HENRY: Then, Richard Earl of Cambridge, there is yours;
There yours, Lord Scroop of Masham; and, Sir Knight,
Grey of Northumberland, this same is yours.
Read them, and know I know your worthiness.
My Lord of Westmoreland, and uncle Exeter,
We will aboard to-night. Why, how now, gentlemen?
What see you in those papers, that you lose
So much complexion? Look ye how they change!
Their cheeks are paper. Why, what read you there
That have so cowarded and chas'd your blood
Out of appearance?

CAMBRIDGE: I do confess my fault,
And do submit me to your Highness' mercy.

GREY, SCROOP: To which we all appeal.

KING HENRY: The mercy that was quick in us but late
By your own counsel is suppress'd and kill'd.
You must not dare, for shame, to talk of mercy;
For your own reasons turn into your bosoms
As dogs upon their masters, worrying you.
See you, my princes and my noble peers,
These English monsters! My Lord of Cambridge here-
You know how apt our love was to accord
To furnish him with an appertinents
Belonging to his honour; and this man

Hath, for a few light crowns, lightly conspir'd,
And sworn unto the practices of France
To kill us here in Hampton; to the which
This knight, no less for bounty bound to us
Than Cambridge is, hath likewise sworn. But, O,
What shall I say to thee, Lord Scroop, thou cruel,
Ingrateful, savage, and inhuman creature?
Thou that didst bear the key of all my counsels,
That knew'st the very bottom of my soul,
That almost mightst have coin'd me into gold,
Wouldst thou have practis'd on me for thy use-
May it be possible that foreign hire
Could out of thee extract one spark of evil
That might annoy my finger? 'Tis so strange
That, though the truth of it stands off as gross
As black and white, my eye will scarcely see it.
Treason and murder ever kept together,
As two yoke-devils sworn to either's purpose,
Working so grossly in a natural cause
That admiration did not whoop at them;
But thou, 'gainst all proportion, didst bring in
Wonder to wait on treason and on murder;
And whatsoever cunning fiend it was
That wrought upon thee so preposterously
Hath got the voice in hell for excellence;
And other devils that suggest by treasons
Do botch and bungle up damnation
With patches, colours, and with forms, being fetch'd
From glist'ring semblances of piety;
But he that temper'd thee bade thee stand up,
Gave thee no instance why thou shouldst do treason,
Unless to dub thee with the name of traitor.
If that same demon that hath gull'd thee thus
Should with his lion gait walk the whole world,
He might return to vasty Tartar back,
And tell the legions 'I can never win
A soul so easy as that Englishman's.'

O, how hast thou with jealousy infected
The sweetness of affiance! Show men dutiful?
Why, so didst thou. Seem they grave and learned?
Why, so didst thou. Come they of noble family?
Why, so didst thou. Seem they religious?
Why, so didst thou. Or are they spare in diet,
Free from gross passion or of mirth or anger,
Constant in spirit, not swerving with the blood,
Garnish'd and deck'd in modest complement,
Not working with the eye without the ear,
And but in purged judgment trusting neither?
Such and so finely bolted didst thou seem;
And thus thy fall hath left a kind of blot
To mark the full-fraught man and best indued
With some suspicion. I will weep for thee;
For this revolt of thine, methinks, is like
Another fall of man. Their faults are open.
Arrest them to the answer of the law;
And God acquit them of their practices!

EXETER: I arrest thee of high treason, by the name of Richard Earl of Cambridge.
I arrest thee of high treason, by the name of Henry Lord Scroop of Masham.
I arrest thee of high treason, by the name of Thomas Grey, knight, of Northumberland.

SCROOP: Our purposes God justly hath discover'd,
And I repent my fault more than my death;
Which I beseech your Highness to forgive,
Although my body pay the price of it.

CAMBRIDGE: For me, the gold of France did not seduce,
Although I did admit it as a motive
The sooner to effect what I intended;
But God be thanked for prevention,
Which I in sufferance heartily will rejoice,
Beseeching God and you to pardon me.

GREY: Never did faithful subject more rejoice
At the discovery of most dangerous treason
Than I do at this hour joy o'er myself,
Prevented from a damned enterprise.
My fault, but not my body, pardon, sovereign.

KING HENRY: God quit you in his mercy! Hear your sentence.
You have conspir'd against our royal person,
Join'd with an enemy proclaim'd, and from his coffers
Receiv'd the golden earnest of our death;
Wherein you would have sold your king to slaughter,
His princes and his peers to servitude,
His subjects to oppression and contempt,
And his whole kingdom into desolation.
Touching our person seek we no revenge;
But we our kingdom's safety must so tender,
Whose ruin you have sought, that to her laws
We do deliver you. Get you therefore hence,
Poor miserable wretches, to your death;
The taste whereof God of his mercy give
You patience to endure, and true repentance
Of all your dear offences. Bear them hence.
Exeunt Cambridge, Scroop, and Grey, guarded
Now, lords, for France; the enterprise whereof
Shall be to you as us like glorious.
We doubt not of a fair and lucky war,
Since God so graciously hath brought to light
This dangerous treason, lurking in our way
To hinder our beginnings; we doubt not now
But every rub is smoothed on our way.
Then, forth, dear countrymen; let us deliver
Our puissance into the hand of God,
Putting it straight in expedition.
Cheerly to sea; the signs of war advance;
No king of England, if not king of France!
Flourish. Exeunt

ACT II. SCENE III. Eastcheap. Before the Boar's Head Tavern

Enter Pistol, Hostess, Nym, Bardolph, and Boy

HOSTESS: Prithee, honey-sweet husband, let me bring thee to Staines.

PISTOL: No; for my manly heart doth earn.
Bardolph, be blithe; Nym, rouse thy vaunting veins;
Boy, bristle thy courage up. For Falstaff he is dead,
And we must earn therefore.

BARDOLPH: Would I were with him, wheresome'er he is, either in heaven or in hell!

HOSTESS: Nay, sure, he's not in hell: he's in Arthur's bosom, if ever man went to Arthur's bosom. 'A made a finer end, and went away an it had been any christom child; 'a parted ev'n just between twelve and one, ev'n at the turning o' th' tide; for after I saw him fumble with the sheets, and play with flowers, and smile upon his fingers' end, I knew there was but one way; for his nose was as sharp as a pen, and 'a babbl'd of green fields. 'How now, Sir John!' quoth I 'What, man, be o' good cheer.' So 'a cried out 'God, God, God!' three or four times. Now I, to comfort him, bid him 'a should not think of God; I hop'd there was no need to trouble himself with any such thoughts yet. So 'a bade me lay more clothes on his feet; I put my hand into the bed and felt them, and they were as cold as any stone; then I felt to his knees, and so upward and upward, and all was as cold as any stone.

NYM: They say he cried out of sack.

HOSTESS: Ay, that 'a did.

BARDOLPH: And of women.

HOSTESS: Nay, that 'a did not.

BOY: Yes, that 'a did, and said they were devils incarnate.

HOSTESS: 'A could never abide carnation; 'twas a colour he never liked.

BOY: 'A said once the devil would have him about women.

HOSTESS: 'A did in some sort, indeed, handle women; but then he was rheumatic, and talk'd of the Whore of Babylon.

BOY: Do you not remember 'a saw a flea stick upon Bardolph's nose, and 'a said it was a black soul burning in hell?

BARDOLPH: Well, the fuel is gone that maintain'd that fire: that's all the riches I got in his service.

NYM: Shall we shog? The King will be gone from Southampton.

PISTOL: Come, let's away. My love, give me thy lips.
Look to my chattles and my moveables;
Let senses rule. The word is 'Pitch and Pay.'
Trust none;
For oaths are straws, men's faiths are wafer-cakes,
And Holdfast is the only dog, my duck.
Therefore, Caveto be thy counsellor.
Go, clear thy crystals. Yoke-fellows in arms,
Let us to France, like horse-leeches, my boys,
To suck, to suck, the very blood to suck.

BOY: And that's but unwholesome food, they say.

PISTOL: Touch her soft mouth and march.

BARDOLPH: Farewell, hostess. *Kissing her*

NYM: I cannot kiss, that is the humour of it; but adieu.

PISTOL: Let housewifery appear; keep close, I thee command.

HOSTESS: Farewell; adieu.
Exeunt

ACT II. SCENE IV. France. The King's Palace

Flourish. Enter the French King, the Dauphin, the Dukes of Berri and Britaine, the Constable, and Others

FRENCH KING: Thus comes the English with full power upon us;
And more than carefully it us concerns
To answer royally in our defences.
Therefore the Dukes of Berri and of Britaine,
Of Brabant and of Orleans, shall make forth,
And you, Prince Dauphin, with all swift dispatch,
To line and new repair our towns of war
With men of courage and with means defendant;
For England his approaches makes as fierce
As waters to the sucking of a gulf.
It fits us, then, to be as provident
As fear may teach us, out of late examples
Left by the fatal and neglected English
Upon our fields.

DAUPHIN: My most redoubted father,
It is most meet we arm us 'gainst the foe;
For peace itself should not so dull a kingdom,
Though war nor no known quarrel were in question,
But that defences, musters, preparations,
Should be maintain'd, assembled, and collected,
As were a war in expectation.
Therefore, I say, 'tis meet we all go forth
To view the sick and feeble parts of France;
And let us do it with no show of fear-
No, with no more than if we heard that England
Were busied with a Whitsun morris-dance;
For, my good liege, she is so idly king'd,
Her sceptre so fantastically borne
By a vain, giddy, shallow, humorous youth,
That fear attends her not.

CONSTABLE: O peace, Prince Dauphin!

You are too much mistaken in this king.
Question your Grace the late ambassadors
With what great state he heard their embassy,
How well supplied with noble counsellors,
How modest in exception, and withal
How terrible in constant resolution,
And you shall find his vanities forespent
Were but the outside of the Roman Brutus,
Covering discretion with a coat of folly;
As gardeners do with ordure hide those roots
That shall first spring and be most delicate.

DAUPHIN: Well, 'tis not so, my Lord High Constable;
But though we think it so, it is no matter.
In cases of defence 'tis best to weigh
The enemy more mighty than he seems;
So the proportions of defence are fill'd;
Which of a weak and niggardly projection
Doth like a miser spoil his coat with scanting
A little cloth.

FRENCH KING: Think we King Harry strong;
And, Princes, look you strongly arm to meet him.
The kindred of him hath been flesh'd upon us;
And he is bred out of that bloody strain
That haunted us in our familiar paths.
Witness our too much memorable shame
When Cressy battle fatally was struck,
And all our princes capdv'd by the hand
Of that black name, Edward, Black Prince of Wales;
Whiles that his mountain sire- on mountain standing,
Up in the air, crown'd with the golden sun-
Saw his heroical seed, and smil'd to see him,
Mangle the work of nature, and deface
The patterns that by God and by French fathers
Had twenty years been made. This is a stern
Of that victorious stock; and let us fear

The native mightiness and fate of him.
Enter a Messenger

MESSENGER: Ambassadors from Harry King of England
Do crave admittance to your Majesty.

FRENCH KING: We'll give them present audience. Go and bring them.
Exeunt Messenger and Certain Lords
You see this chase is hotly followed, friends.

DAUPHIN: Turn head and stop pursuit; for coward dogs
Most spend their mouths when what they seem to threaten
Runs far before them. Good my sovereign,
Take up the English short, and let them know
Of what a monarchy you are the head.
Self-love, my liege, is not so vile a sin
As self-neglecting.
Re-enter Lords, with Exeter and Train

FRENCH KING: From our brother of England?

EXETER: From him, and thus he greets your Majesty:
He wills you, in the name of God Almighty,
That you divest yourself, and lay apart
The borrowed glories that by gift of heaven,
By law of nature and of nations, 'longs
To him and to his heirs- namely, the crown,
And all wide-stretched honours that pertain,
By custom and the ordinance of times,
Unto the crown of France. That you may know
'Tis no sinister nor no awkward claim,
Pick'd from the worm-holes of long-vanish'd days,
Nor from the dust of old oblivion rak'd,
He sends you this most memorable line, *Gives a Paper*
In every branch truly demonstrative;
Willing you overlook this pedigree.
And when you find him evenly deriv'd

From his most fam'd of famous ancestors,
Edward the Third, he bids you then resign
Your crown and kingdom, indirectly held
From him, the native and true challenger.

FRENCH KING: Or else what follows?

EXETER: Bloody constraint; for if you hide the crown
Even in your hearts, there will he rake for it.
Therefore in fierce tempest is he coming,
In thunder and in earthquake, like a Jove,
That if requiring fail, he will compel;
And bids you, in the bowels of the Lord,
Deliver up the crown; and to take mercy
On the poor souls for whom this hungry war
Opens his vasty jaws; and on your head
Turning the widows' tears, the orphans' cries,
The dead men's blood, the privy maidens' groans,
For husbands, fathers, and betrothed lovers,
That shall be swallowed in this controversy.
This is his claim, his threat'ning, and my message;
Unless the Dauphin be in presence here,
To whom expressly I bring greeting too.

FRENCH KING: For us, we will consider of this further;
To-morrow shall you bear our full intent
Back to our brother of England.

DAUPHIN: For the Dauphin:
I stand here for him. What to him from England?

EXETER: Scorn and defiance, slight regard, contempt,
And anything that may not misbecome
The mighty sender, doth he prize you at.
Thus says my king: an if your father's Highness
Do not, in grant of all demands at large,
Sweeten the bitter mock you sent his Majesty,

He'll call you to so hot an answer of it
That caves and womby vaultages of France
Shall chide your trespass and return your mock
In second accent of his ordinance.

DAUPHIN: Say, if my father render fair return,
It is against my will; for I desire
Nothing but odds with England. To that end,
As matching to his youth and vanity,
I did present him with the Paris balls.

EXETER: He'll make your Paris Louvre shake for it,
Were it the mistress court of mighty Europe;
And be assur'd you'll find a difference,
As we his subjects have in wonder found,
Between the promise of his greener days
And these he masters now. Now he weighs time
Even to the utmost grain; that you shall read
In your own losses, if he stay in France.

FRENCH KING: To-morrow shall you know our mind at full.

EXETER: Dispatch us with all speed, lest that our king
Come here himself to question our delay;
For he is footed in this land already.

FRENCH KING: You shall be soon dispatch'd with fair conditions.
A night is but small breath and little pause
To answer matters of this consequence.
Flourish. Exeunt

ACT III. PROLOGUE. Flourish. Enter Chorus

CHORUS: Thus with imagin'd wing our swift scene flies,
In motion of no less celerity
Than that of thought. Suppose that you have seen
The well-appointed King at Hampton pier

Embark his royalty; and his brave fleet
With silken streamers the young Phorbus fanning.
Play with your fancies; and in them behold
Upon the hempen tackle ship-boys climbing;
Hear the shrill whistle which doth order give
To sounds confus'd; behold the threaden sails,
Borne with th' invisible and creeping wind,
Draw the huge bottoms through the furrowed sea,
Breasting the lofty surge. O, do but think
You stand upon the rivage and behold
A city on th' inconstant billows dancing;
For so appears this fleet majestical,
Holding due course to Harfleur. Follow, follow!
Grapple your minds to sternage of this navy
And leave your England as dead midnight still,
Guarded with grandsires, babies, and old women,
Either past or not arriv'd to pith and puissance;
For who is he whose chin is but enrich'd
With one appearing hair that will not follow
These cull'd and choice-drawn cavaliers to France?
Work, work your thoughts, and therein see a siege;
Behold the ordnance on their carriages,
With fatal mouths gaping on girded Harfleur.
Suppose th' ambassador from the French comes back;
Tells Harry that the King doth offer him
Katherine his daughter, and with her to dowry
Some petty and unprofitable dukedoms.
The offer likes not; and the nimble gunner
With linstock now the devilish cannon touches,
Alarum, and Chambers Go Off
And down goes an before them. Still be kind,
And eke out our performance with your mind. *Exit*

ACT III. SCENE I. France. Before Harfleur

Alarum. Enter the King, Exeter, Bedford, Gloucester, and Soldiers with Scaling-ladders

KING: Once more unto the breach, dear friends, once more;
Or close the wall up with our English dead.
In peace there's nothing so becomes a man
As modest stillness and humility;
But when the blast of war blows in our ears,
Then imitate the action of the tiger:
Stiffen the sinews, summon up the blood,
Disguise fair nature with hard-favour'd rage;
Then lend the eye a terrible aspect;
Let it pry through the portage of the head
Like the brass cannon: let the brow o'erwhelm it
As fearfully as doth a galled rock
O'erhang and jutty his confounded base,
Swill'd with the wild and wasteful ocean.
Now set the teeth and stretch the nostril wide;
Hold hard the breath, and bend up every spirit
To his full height. On, on, you noblest English,
Whose blood is fet from fathers of war-proof-
Fathers that like so many Alexanders
Have in these parts from morn till even fought,
And sheath'd their swords for lack of argument.
Dishonour not your mothers; now attest
That those whom you call'd fathers did beget you.
Be copy now to men of grosser blood,
And teach them how to war. And you, good yeomen,
Whose limbs were made in England, show us here
The mettle of your pasture; let us swear
That you are worth your breeding- which I doubt not;
For there is none of you so mean and base
That hath not noble lustre in your eyes.
I see you stand like greyhounds in the slips,
Straining upon the start. The game's afoot:
Follow your spirit; and upon this charge

Cry 'God for Harry, England, and Saint George!'
Exeunt. Alarum, and Chambers Go Off

ACT III. SCENE II. Before Harfleur

Enter Nym, Bardolph, Pistol, and Boy

BARDOLPH: On, on, on, on, on! to the breach, to the breach!

NYM: Pray thee, Corporal, stay; the knocks are too hot, and for mine own part I have not a case of lives. The humour of it is too hot; that is the very plain-song of it.

PISTOL: The plain-song is most just; for humours do abound:
Knocks go and come; God's vassals drop and die;
And sword and shield
In bloody field
Doth win immortal fame.

BOY: Would I were in an alehouse in London! I wouid give all my fame for a pot of ale and safety.

PISTOL: And I:
If wishes would prevail with me,
My purpose should not fail with me,
But thither would I hie.

BOY: As duly, but not as truly,
As bird doth sing on bough.
Enter Fluellen

FLUELLEN: Up to the breach, you dogs!
Avaunt, you cullions! *Driving Them Forward*

PISTOL: Be merciful, great duke, to men of mould.
Abate thy rage, abate thy manly rage;
Abate thy rage, great duke.
Good bawcock, bate thy rage. Use lenity, sweet chuck.

NYM: These be good humours. Your honour wins bad humours.
Exeunt All but Boy

BOY: As young as I am, I have observ'd these three swashers. I am boy to them all three; but all they three, though they would serve me, could not be man to me; for indeed three such antics do not amount to a man. For Bardolph, he is white-liver'd and red-fac'd; by the means whereof 'a faces it out, but fights not. For Pistol, he hath a killing tongue and a quiet sword; by the means whereof 'a breaks words and keeps whole weapons. For Nym, he hath heard that men of few words are the best men, and therefore he scorns to say his prayers lest 'a should be thought a coward; but his few bad words are match'd with as few good deeds; for 'a never broke any man's head but his own, and that was against a post when he was drunk. They will steal anything, and call it purchase. Bardolph stole a lute-case, bore it twelve leagues, and sold it for three halfpence. Nym and Bardolph are sworn brothers in filching, and in Calais they stole a fire-shovel; I knew by that piece of service the men would carry coals. They would have me as familiar with men's pockets as their gloves or their handkerchers; which makes much against my manhood, if I should take from another's pocket to put into mine; for it is plain pocketing up of wrongs. I must leave them and seek some better service; their villainy goes against my weak stomach, and therefore I must cast it up.
Exit
Re-enter Fluellen, Gower Following

GOWER: Captain Fluellen, you must come presently to the mines; the Duke of Gloucester would speak with you.

FLUELLEN: To the mines! Tell you the Duke it is not so good to come to the mines; for, look you, the mines is not according to the disciplines of the war; the concavities of it is not sufficient. For, look you, th' athversary- you may discuss unto the Duke, look you- is digt himself four yard under the countermines; by Cheshu, I think 'a will plow up all, if there is not better directions.

GOWER: The Duke of Gloucester, to whom the order of the siege is given, is altogether directed by an Irishman- a very vallant gentleman, i' faith.

FLUELLEN: It is Captain Macmorris, is it not?

GOWER: I think it be.

FLUELLEN: By Cheshu, he is an ass, as in the world: I will verify as much in his beard; he has no more directions in the true disciplines of the wars, look you, of the Roman disciplines, than is a puppy-dog.

Enter Macmorris and Captain Jamy

GOWER: Here 'a comes; and the Scots captain, Captain Jamy, with him.

FLUELLEN: Captain Jamy is a marvellous falorous gentleman, that is certain, and of great expedition and knowledge in th' aunchient wars, upon my particular knowledge of his directions. By Cheshu, he will maintain his argument as well as any military man in the world, in the disciplines of the pristine wars of the Romans.

JAMY: I say gud day, Captain Fluellen.

FLUELLEN: God-den to your worship, good Captain James.

GOWER: How now, Captain Macmorris! Have you quit the mines? Have the pioneers given o'er?

MACMORRIS: By Chrish, la, tish ill done! The work ish give over, the trompet sound the retreat. By my hand, I swear, and my father's soul, the work ish ill done; it ish give over; I would have blowed up the town, so Chrish save me, la, in an hour. O, tish ill done, tish ill done; by my hand, tish ill done!

FLUELLEN: Captain Macmorris, I beseech you now, will you voutsafe me, look you, a few disputations with you, as partly touching or concerning the disciplines of the war, the Roman wars, in the way of argument, look you, and friendly communication; partly to satisfy my opinion, and partly for the satisfaction, look you, of my mind, as touching the direction of the military discipline, that is the point.

JAMY: It sall be vary gud, gud feith, gud captains bath; and I sall quit you with gud leve, as I may pick occasion; that sall I, marry.

MACMORRIS: It is no time to discourse, so Chrish save me. The day is hot, and the weather, and the wars, and the King, and the Dukes; it is no time to discourse. The town is beseech'd, and the trumpet call us to the breach; and we talk and, be Chrish, do nothing. 'Tis shame for us all, so God sa' me, 'tis shame to stand still; it is shame, by my hand; and there is throats to be cut, and works to be done; and there ish nothing done, so Chrish sa' me, la.

JAMY: By the mess, ere theise eyes of mine take themselves to slomber, ay'll de gud service, or I'll lig i' th' grund for it; ay, or go to death. And I'll pay't as valorously as I may, that sall I suerly do, that is the breff and the long. Marry, I wad full fain heard some question 'tween you tway.

FLUELLEN: Captain Macmorris, I think, look you, under your correction, there is not many of your nation-

MACMORRIS: Of my nation? What ish my nation? Ish a villain, and a bastard, and a knave, and a rascal. What ish my nation? Who talks of my nation?

FLUELLEN: Look you, if you take the matter otherwise than is meant, Captain Macmorris, peradventure I shall think you do not use me with that affability as in discretion you ought to use me, look you; being as good a man as yourself, both in the disciplines of war and in the derivation of my birth, and in other particularities.

MACMORRIS: I do not know you so good a man as myself; so Chrish save me, I will cut off your head.

GOWER: Gentlemen both, you will mistake each other.

JAMY: Ah! that's a foul fault.
A Parley Sounded

GOWER: The town sounds a parley.

FLUELLEN: Captain Macmorris, when there is more better opportunity to be required, look you, I will be so bold as to tell you I know the disciplines of war; and there is an end.

Exeunt

ACT III. SCENE III. Before the Gates of Harfleur

Enter the Governor and Some Citizens on the Walls. Enter the King and All His Train Before the Gates

KING HENRY: How yet resolves the Governor of the town?
This is the latest parle we will admit;
Therefore to our best mercy give yourselves
Or, like to men proud of destruction,
Defy us to our worst; for, as I am a soldier,
A name that in my thoughts becomes me best,
If I begin the batt'ry once again,
I will not leave the half-achieved Harfleur
Till in her ashes she lie buried.
The gates of mercy shall be all shut up,
And the flesh'd soldier, rough and hard of heart,
In liberty of bloody hand shall range
With conscience wide as hell, mowing like grass
Your fresh fair virgins and your flow'ring infants.
What is it then to me if impious war,
Array'd in flames, like to the prince of fiends,
Do, with his smirch'd complexion, all fell feats
Enlink'd to waste and desolation?
What is't to me when you yourselves are cause,
If your pure maidens fall into the hand
Of hot and forcing violation?
What rein can hold licentious wickednes
When down the hill he holds his fierce career?
We may as bootless spend our vain command
Upon th' enraged soldiers in their spoil,
As send precepts to the Leviathan
To come ashore. Therefore, you men of Harfleur,
Take pity of your town and of your people

Whiles yet my soldiers are in my command;
Whiles yet the cool and temperate wind of grace
O'erblows the filthy and contagious clouds
Of heady murder, spoil, and villainy.
If not- why, in a moment look to see
The blind and bloody with foul hand
Defile the locks of your shrill-shrieking daughters;
Your fathers taken by the silver beards,
And their most reverend heads dash'd to the walls;
Your naked infants spitted upon pikes,
Whiles the mad mothers with their howls confus'd
Do break the clouds, as did the wives of Jewry
At Herod's bloody-hunting slaughtermen.
What say you? Will you yield, and this avoid?
Or, guilty in defence, be thus destroy'd?

GOVERNOR: Our expectation hath this day an end:
The Dauphin, whom of succours we entreated,
Returns us that his powers are yet not ready
To raise so great a siege. Therefore, great King,
We yield our town and lives to thy soft mercy.
Enter our gates; dispose of us and ours;
For we no longer are defensible.

KING HENRY: Open your gates.
Exit Governor
Come, uncle Exeter,
Go you and enter Harfleur; there remain,
And fortify it strongly 'gainst the French;
Use mercy to them all. For us, dear uncle,
The winter coming on, and sickness growing
Upon our soldiers, we will retire to Calais.
To-night in Harfleur will we be your guest;
To-morrow for the march are we addrest.
Flourish. The King and His Train Enter the Town

ACT III. SCENE IV. Rouen. The French King's Palace

Enter Katherine and Alice

KATHERINE: Alice, tu as ete en Angleterre, et tu parles bien le langage.

ALICE: Un peu, madame.

KATHERINE: Je te prie, m'enseignez; il faut que j'apprenne a parler. Comment appelez-vous la main en Anglais?

ALICE: La main? Elle est appelee de hand.

KATHERINE: De hand. Et les doigts?

ALICE: Les doigts? Ma foi, j'oublie les doigts; mais je me souviendrai. Les doigts? Je pense qu'ils sont appeles de fingres; oui, de fingres.

KATHERINE: La main, de hand; les doigts, de fingres. Je pense que je suis le bon ecolier; j'ai gagne deux mots d'Anglais vitement. Comment appelez-vous les ongles?

ALICE: Les ongles? Nous les appelons de nails.

KATHERINE: De nails. Ecoutez; dites-moi si je parle bien: de hand, de fingres, et de nails.

ALICE: C'est bien dit, madame; il est fort bon Anglais.

KATHERINE: Dites-moi l'Anglais pour le bras.

ALICE: De arm, madame.

KATHERINE: Et le coude?

ALICE: D'elbow.

KATHERINE: D'elbow. Je m'en fais la repetition de tous les mots que vous m'avez appris des a present.

ALICE: Il est trop difficile, madame, comme je pense.

KATHERINE: Excusez-moi, Alice; ecoutez: d'hand, de fingre, de nails, d'arma, de bilbow.

ALICE: D'elbow, madame.

KATHERINE: O Seigneur Dieu, je m'en oublie! D'elbow.
Comment appelez-vous le col?

ALICE: De nick, madame.

KATHERINE: De nick. Et le menton?

ALICE: De chin.

KATHERINE: De sin. Le col, de nick; le menton, de sin.

ALICE: Oui. Sauf votre honneur, en verite, vous prononcez les mots aussi droit que les natifs d'Angleterre.

KATHERINE: Je ne doute point d'apprendre, par la grace de Dieu, et en peu de temps.

ALICE: N'avez-vous pas deja oublie ce que je vous ai enseigne?

KATHERINE: Non, je reciterai a vous promptement: d'hand, de fingre, de mails-

ALICE: De nails, madame.

KATHERINE: De nails, de arm, de ilbow.

ALICE: Sauf votre honneur, d'elbow.

KATHERINE: Ainsi dis-je; d'elbow, de nick, et de sin. Comment appelez-vous le pied et la robe?

ALICE: Le foot, madame; et le count.

KATHERINE: Le foot et le count. O Seigneur Dieu! ils sont mots de son mauvais, corruptible, gros, et impudique, et non pour les dames d'honneur d'user: je ne voudrais prononcer ces mots devant les seigneurs de France pour tout le monde. Foh! le foot et le count! Neanmoins, je reciterai une autre fois ma lecon ensemble: d'hand, de fingre, de nails, d'arm, d'elbow, de nick, de sin, de foot, le count.

ALICE: Excellent, madame!

KATHERINE: C'est assez pour une fois: allons-nous a diner.
Exeunt

ACT III. SCENE V. The French King's Palace

Enter the King of France, the Dauphin, Duke of Britaine, the Constable of France, and Others

FRENCH KING: 'Tis certain he hath pass'd the river Somme.

CONSTABLE: And if he be not fought withal, my lord,
Let us not live in France; let us quit an,
And give our vineyards to a barbarous people.

DAUPHIN: O Dieu vivant! Shall a few sprays of us,
The emptying of our fathers' luxury,
Our scions, put in wild and savage stock,
Spirt up so suddenly into the clouds,
And overlook their grafters?

BRITAINE: Normans, but bastard Normans, Norman bastards!
Mort Dieu, ma vie! if they march along
Unfought withal, but I will sell my dukedom
To buy a slobb'ry and a dirty farm

In that nook-shotten isle of Albion.

CONSTABLE: Dieu de batailles! where have they this mettle?
Is not their climate foggy, raw, and dull;
On whom, as in despite, the sun looks pale,
Killing their fruit with frowns? Can sodden water,
A drench for sur-rein'd jades, their barley-broth,
Decoct their cold blood to such valiant heat?
And shall our quick blood, spirited with wine,
Seem frosty? O, for honour of our land,
Let us not hang like roping icicles
Upon our houses' thatch, whiles a more frosty people
Sweat drops of gallant youth in our rich fields-
Poor we call them in their native lords!

DAUPHIN: By faith and honour,
Our madams mock at us and plainly say
Our mettle is bred out, and they will give
Their bodies to the lust of English youth
To new-store France with bastard warriors.

BRITAINE: They bid us to the English dancing-schools
And teach lavoltas high and swift corantos,
Saying our grace is only in our heels
And that we are most lofty runaways.

FRENCH KING: Where is Montjoy the herald? Speed him hence;
Let him greet England with our sharp defiance.
Up, Princes, and, with spirit of honour edged
More sharper than your swords, hie to the field:
Charles Delabreth, High Constable of France;
You Dukes of Orleans, Bourbon, and of Berri,
Alengon, Brabant, Bar, and Burgundy;
Jaques Chatillon, Rambures, Vaudemont,
Beaumont, Grandpre, Roussi, and Fauconbridge,
Foix, Lestrake, Bouciqualt, and Charolois;
High dukes, great princes, barons, lords, and knights,

For your great seats now quit you of great shames.
Bar Harry England, that sweeps through our land
With pennons painted in the blood of Harfleur.
Rush on his host as doth the melted snow
Upon the valleys, whose low vassal seat
The Alps doth spit and void his rheum upon;
Go down upon him, you have power enough,
And in a captive chariot into Rouen
Bring him our prisoner.

CONSTABLE: This becomes the great.
Sorry am I his numbers are so few,
His soldiers sick and famish'd in their march;
For I am sure, when he shall see our army,
He'll drop his heart into the sink of fear,
And for achievement offer us his ransom.

FRENCH KING: Therefore, Lord Constable, haste on Montjoy,
And let him say to England that we send
To know what willing ransom he will give.
Prince Dauphin, you shall stay with us in Rouen.

DAUPHIN: Not so, I do beseech your Majesty.

FRENCH KING: Be patient, for you shall remain with us.
Now forth, Lord Constable and Princes all,
And quickly bring us word of England's fall.
Exeunt

ACT III. SCENE VI. The English Camp in Picardy

Enter Captains, English and Welsh, Gower and Fluellen

GOWER: How now, Captain Fluellen! Come you from the bridge?

FLUELLEN: I assure you there is very excellent services committed at the bridge.

GOWER: Is the Duke of Exeter safe?

FLUELLEN: The Duke of Exeter is as magnanimous as Agamemnon; and a man that I love and honour with my soul, and my heart, and my duty, and my live, and my living, and my uttermost power. He is not- God be praised and blessed!- any hurt in the world, but keeps the bridge most valiantly, with excellent discipline. There is an aunchient Lieutenant there at the bridge- I think in my very conscience he is as valiant a man as Mark Antony; and he is man of no estimation in the world; but I did see him do as gallant service.

GOWER: What do you call him?

FLUELLEN: He is call'd Aunchient Pistol.

GOWER: I know him not.
Enter Pistol

FLUELLEN: Here is the man.

PISTOL: Captain, I thee beseech to do me favours.
The Duke of Exeter doth love thee well.

FLUELLEN: Ay, I praise God; and I have merited some love at his hands.

PISTOL: Bardolph, a soldier, firm and sound of heart,
And of buxom valour, hath by cruel fate
And giddy Fortune's furious fickle wheel,
That goddess blind,
That stands upon the rolling restless stone-

FLUELLEN: By your patience, Aunchient Pistol. Fortune is painted blind, with a muffler afore her eyes, to signify to you that Fortune is blind; and she is painted also with a wheel, to signify to you, which is the moral of it, that she is turning, and inconstant, and mutability, and variation; and her foot, look you, is fixed upon a spherical stone, which rolls, and rolls, and rolls. In good truth, the poet makes a most excellent description of it: Fortune is an excellent moral.

PISTOL: Fortune is Bardolph's foe, and frowns on him;
For he hath stol'n a pax, and hanged must 'a be-
A damned death!
Let gallows gape for dog; let man go free,
And let not hemp his windpipe suffocate.
But Exeter hath given the doom of death
For pax of little price.
Therefore, go speak- the Duke will hear thy voice;
And let not Bardolph's vital thread be cut
With edge of penny cord and vile reproach.
Speak, Captain, for his life, and I will thee requite.

FLUELLEN: Aunchient Pistol, I do partly understand your meaning.

PISTOL: Why then, rejoice therefore.

FLUELLEN: Certainly, Aunchient, it is not a thing to rejoice at; for if, look you, he were my brother, I would desire the Duke to use his good pleasure, and put him to execution; for discipline ought to be used.

PISTOL: Die and be damn'd! and figo for thy friendship!

FLUELLEN: It is well.

PISTOL: The fig of Spain!
Exit

FLUELLEN: Very good.

GOWER: Why, this is an arrant counterfeit rascal; I remember him now- a bawd, a cutpurse.

FLUELLEN: I'll assure you, 'a utt'red as prave words at the pridge as you shall see in a summer's day. But it is very well; what he has spoke to me, that is well, I warrant you, when time is serve.

GOWER: Why, 'tis a gull a fool a rogue, that now and then goes to the wars to grace himself, at his return into London, under the form of a soldier. And such fellows are perfect in the great commanders' names; and they will learn you by rote where services were done- at such and such a sconce, at such a breach, at such a convoy; who came off bravely, who was shot, who disgrac'd, what terms the enemy stood on; and this they con perfectly in the phrase of war, which they trick up with new-tuned oaths; and what a beard of the General's cut and a horrid suit of the camp will do among foaming bottles and ale-wash'd wits is wonderful to be thought on. But you must learn to know such slanders of the age, or else you may be marvellously mistook.

FLUELLEN: I tell you what, Captain Gower, I do perceive he is not the man that he would gladly make show to the world he is; if I find a hole in his coat I will tell him my mind. *Drum Within* Hark you, the King is coming; and I must speak with him from the pridge.

Drum and Colours. Enter the King and His Poor Soldiers, and Gloucester

God pless your Majesty!

KING HENRY: How now, Fluellen! Cam'st thou from the bridge?

FLUELLEN: Ay, so please your Majesty. The Duke of Exeter has very gallantly maintain'd the pridge; the French is gone off, look you, and there is gallant and most prave passages. Marry, th' athversary was have possession of the pridge; but he is enforced to retire, and the Duke of Exeter is master of the pridge; I can tell your Majesty the Duke is a prave man.

KING HENRY: What men have you lost, Fluellen!

FLUELLEN: The perdition of th' athversary hath been very great, reasonable great; marry, for my part, I think the Duke hath lost never a man, but one that is like to be executed for robbing a church- one Bardolph, if your Majesty know the man; his face is all bubukles, and whelks, and knobs, and flames o' fire; and his lips blows at his nose, and it is like a coal of fire, sometimes plue and sometimes red; but his nose is executed and his fire's out.

KING HENRY: We would have all such offenders so cut off. And we give express charge that in our marches through the country there be nothing compell'd from the villages, nothing taken but paid for, none of the French upbraided or abused in disdainful language; for when lenity and cruelty play for a kingdom the gentler gamester is the soonest winner.

Tucket. Enter Montjoy

MONTJOY: You know me by my habit.

KING HENRY: Well then, I know thee; what shall I know of thee?

MONTJOY: My master's mind.

KING HENRY: Unfold it.

MONTJOY: Thus says my king. Say thou to Harry of England: Though we seem'd dead we did but sleep; advantage is a better soldier than rashness. Tell him we could have rebuk'd him at Harfleur, but that we thought not good to bruise an injury till it were full ripe. Now we speak upon our cue, and our voice is imperial: England shall repent his folly, see his weakness, and admire our sufferance. Bid him therefore consider of his ransom, which must proportion the losses we have borne, the subjects we have lost, the disgrace we have digested; which, in weight to re-answer, his pettiness would bow under. For our losses his exchequer is too poor; for th' effusion of our blood, the muster of his kingdom too faint a number; and for our disgrace, his own person kneeling at our feet but a weak and worthless satisfaction. To this add defiance; and tell him, for conclusion, he hath betrayed his followers, whose condemnation is pronounc'd. So far my king and master; so much my office.

KING HENRY: What is thy name? I know thy quality.

MONTJOY: Montjoy.

KING HENRY: Thou dost thy office fairly. Turn thee back,
And tell thy king I do not seek him now,
But could be willing to march on to Calais
Without impeachment; for, to say the sooth-
Though 'tis no wisdom to confess so much
Unto an enemy of craft and vantage-

My people are with sickness much enfeebled;
My numbers lessen'd; and those few I have
Almost no better than so many French;
Who when they were in health, I tell thee, herald,
I thought upon one pair of English legs
Did march three Frenchmen. Yet forgive me, God,
That I do brag thus; this your air of France
Hath blown that vice in me; I must repent.
Go, therefore, tell thy master here I am;
My ransom is this frail and worthless trunk;
My army but a weak and sickly guard;
Yet, God before, tell him we will come on,
Though France himself and such another neighbour
Stand in our way. There's for thy labour, Montjoy.
Go, bid thy master well advise himself.
If we may pass, we will; if we be hind'red,
We shall your tawny ground with your red blood
Discolour; and so, Montjoy, fare you well.
The sum of all our answer is but this:
We would not seek a battle as we are;
Nor as we are, we say, we will not shun it.
So tell your master.

MONTJOY: I shall deliver so. Thanks to your Highness.
Exit

GLOUCESTER: I hope they will not come upon us now.

KING HENRY: We are in God's hand, brother, not in theirs.
March to the bridge, it now draws toward night;
Beyond the river we'll encamp ourselves,
And on to-morrow bid them march away.
Exeunt

ACT III. SCENE VII. The French Camp near Agincourt

Enter the Constable of France, the Lord Rambures, the Duke of Orleans, the Dauphin, with Others

CONSTABLE: Tut! I have the best armour of the world.
Would it were day!

ORLEANS: You have an excellent armour; but let my horse have his due.

CONSTABLE: It is the best horse of Europe.

ORLEANS: Will it never be morning?

DAUPHIN: My Lord of Orleans and my Lord High Constable, you talk of horse and armour?

ORLEANS: You are as well provided of both as any prince in the world.

DAUPHIN: What a long night is this! I will not change my horse with any that treads but on four pasterns. Ca, ha! he bounds from the earth as if his entrails were hairs; le cheval volant, the Pegasus, chez les narines de feu! When I bestride him I soar, I am a hawk. He trots the air; the earth sings when he touches it; the basest horn of his hoof is more musical than the pipe of Hermes.

ORLEANS: He's of the colour of the nutmeg.

DAUPHIN: And of the heat of the ginger. It is a beast for Perseus: he is pure air and fire; and the dull elements of earth and water never appear in him, but only in patient stillness while his rider mounts him; he is indeed a horse, and all other jades you may call beasts.

CONSTABLE: Indeed, my lord, it is a most absolute and excellent horse.

DAUPHIN: It is the prince of palfreys; his neigh is like the bidding of a monarch, and his countenance enforces homage.

ORLEANS: No more, cousin.

DAUPHIN: Nay, the man hath no wit that cannot, from the rising of the lark to the lodging of the lamb, vary deserved praise on my palfrey. It is a theme as fluent as the sea: turn the sands into eloquent tongues, and my horse is argument for them all: 'tis a subject for a sovereign to reason on, and for a sovereign's sovereign to ride on; and for the world- familiar to us and unknown- to lay apart their particular functions and wonder at him. I once writ a sonnet in his praise and began thus: 'Wonder of nature'-

ORLEANS: I have heard a sonnet begin so to one's mistress.

DAUPHIN: Then did they imitate that which I compos'd to my courser; for my horse is my mistress.

ORLEANS: Your mistress bears well.

DAUPHIN: Me well; which is the prescript praise and perfection of a good and particular mistress.

CONSTABLE: Nay, for methought yesterday your mistress shrewdly shook your back.

DAUPHIN: So perhaps did yours.

CONSTABLE: Mine was not bridled.

DAUPHIN: O, then belike she was old and gentle; and you rode like a kern of Ireland, your French hose off and in your strait strossers.

CONSTABLE: You have good judgment in horsemanship.

DAUPHIN: Be warn'd by me, then: they that ride so, and ride not warily, fall into foul bogs. I had rather have my horse to my mistress.

CONSTABLE: I had as lief have my mistress a jade.

DAUPHIN: I tell thee, Constable, my mistress wears his own hair.

CONSTABLE: I could make as true a boast as that, if I had a sow to my mistress.

DAUPHIN: 'Le chien est retourne a son propre vomissement, et la truie lavee au bourbier.' Thou mak'st use of anything.

CONSTABLE: Yet do I not use my horse for my mistress, or any such proverb so little kin to the purpose.

RAMBURES: My Lord Constable, the armour that I saw in your tent to-night- are those stars or suns upon it?

CONSTABLE: Stars, my lord.

DAUPHIN: Some of them will fall to-morrow, I hope.

CONSTABLE: And yet my sky shall not want.

DAUPHIN: That may be, for you bear a many superfluously, and 'twere more honour some were away.

CONSTABLE: Ev'n as your horse bears your praises, who would trot as well were some of your brags dismounted.

DAUPHIN: Would I were able to load him with his desert! Will it never be day? I will trot to-morrow a mile, and my way shall be paved with English faces.

CONSTABLE: I will not say so, for fear I should be fac'd out of my way; but I would it were morning, for I would fain be about the ears of the English.

RAMBURES: Who will go to hazard with me for twenty prisoners?

CONSTABLE: You must first go yourself to hazard ere you have them.

DAUPHIN: 'Tis midnight; I'll go arm myself.
Exit

ORLEANS: The Dauphin longs for morning.

RAMBURES: He longs to eat the English.

CONSTABLE: I think he will eat all he kills.

ORLEANS: By the white hand of my lady, he's a gallant prince.

CONSTABLE: Swear by her foot, that she may tread out the oath.

ORLEANS: He is simply the most active gentleman of France.

CONSTABLE: Doing is activity, and he will still be doing.

ORLEANS: He never did harm that I heard of.

CONSTABLE: Nor will do none to-morrow: he will keep that good name still.

ORLEANS: I know him to be valiant.

CONSTABLE: I was told that by one that knows him better than you.

ORLEANS: What's he?

CONSTABLE: Marry, he told me so himself; and he said he car'd not who knew it.

ORLEANS: He needs not; it is no hidden virtue in him.

CONSTABLE: By my faith, sir, but it is; never anybody saw it but his lackey.
'Tis a hooded valour, and when it appears it will bate.

ORLEANS: Ill-wind never said well.

CONSTABLE: I will cap that proverb with 'There is flattery in friendship.'

ORLEANS: And I will take up that with 'Give the devil his due.'

CONSTABLE: Well plac'd! There stands your friend for the devil; have at the very eye of that proverb with 'A pox of the devil!'

ORLEANS: You are the better at proverbs by how much 'A fool's bolt is soon shot.'

CONSTABLE: You have shot over.

ORLEANS: 'Tis not the first time you were overshot.
Enter a Messenger

MESSENGER: My Lord High Constable, the English lie within fifteen hundred paces of your tents.

CONSTABLE: Who hath measur'd the ground?

MESSENGER: The Lord Grandpre.

CONSTABLE: A valiant and most expert gentleman. Would it were day! Alas, poor Harry of England! he longs not for the dawning as we do.

ORLEANS: What a wretched and peevish fellow is this King of England, to mope with his fat-brain'd followers so far out of his knowledge!

CONSTABLE: If the English had any apprehension, they would run away.

ORLEANS: That they lack; for if their heads had any intellectual armour, they could never wear such heavy head-pieces.

RAMBURES: That island of England breeds very valiant creatures; their mastiffs are of unmatchable courage.

ORLEANS: Foolish curs, that run winking into the mouth of a Russian bear, and have their heads crush'd like rotten apples! You may as well say that's a valiant flea that dare eat his breakfast on the lip of a lion.

CONSTABLE: Just, just! and the men do sympathise with the mastiffs in robustious and rough coming on, leaving their wits with their wives; and then give them great meals of beef and iron and steel; they will eat like wolves and fight like devils.

ORLEANS: Ay, but these English are shrewdly out of beef.

CONSTABLE: Then shall we find to-morrow they have only stomachs to eat, and none to fight. Now is it time to arm. Come, shall we about it?

ORLEANS: It is now two o'clock; but let me see- by ten
We shall have each a hundred Englishmen.
Exeunt

ACT IV. PROLOGUE. Enter Chorus

CHORUS: Now entertain conjecture of a time
When creeping murmur and the poring dark
Fills the wide vessel of the universe.
From camp to camp, through the foul womb of night,
The hum of either army stilly sounds,
That the fix'd sentinels almost receive
The secret whispers of each other's watch.
Fire answers fire, and through their paly flames
Each battle sees the other's umber'd face;
Steed threatens steed, in high and boastful neighs
Piercing the night's dull ear; and from the tents
The armourers accomplishing the knights,
With busy hammers closing rivets up,
Give dreadful note of preparation.
The country cocks do crow, the clocks do ton,
And the third hour of drowsy morning name.
Proud of their numbers and secure in soul,

The confident and over-lusty French
Do the low-rated English play at dice;
And chide the cripple tardy-gaited night
Who like a foul and ugly witch doth limp
So tediously away. The poor condemned English,
Like sacrifices, by their watchful fires
Sit patiently and inly ruminate
The morning's danger; and their gesture sad
Investing lank-lean cheeks and war-worn coats
Presenteth them unto the gazing moon
So many horrid ghosts. O, now, who will behold
The royal captain of this ruin'd band
Walking from watch to watch, from tent to tent,
Let him cry 'Praise and glory on his head!'
For forth he goes and visits all his host;
Bids them good morrow with a modest smile,
And calls them brothers, friends, and countrymen.
Upon his royal face there is no note
How dread an army hath enrounded him;
Nor doth he dedicate one jot of colour
Unto the weary and all-watched night;
But freshly looks, and over-bears attaint
With cheerful semblance and sweet majesty;
That every wretch, pining and pale before,
Beholding him, plucks comfort from his looks;
A largess universal, like the sun,
His liberal eye doth give to every one,
Thawing cold fear, that mean and gentle all
Behold, as may unworthiness define,
A little touch of Harry in the night.
And so our scene must to the battle fly;
Where- O for pity!- we shall much disgrace
With four or five most vile and ragged foils,
Right ill-dispos'd in brawl ridiculous,
The name of Agincourt. Yet sit and see,
Minding true things by what their mock'ries be.
Exit

ACT IV. SCENE I. France. The English Camp at Agincourt

Enter the King, Bedford, and Gloucester

KING HENRY: Gloucester, 'tis true that we are in great danger;
The greater therefore should our courage be.
Good morrow, brother Bedford. God Almighty!
There is some soul of goodness in things evil,
Would men observingly distil it out;
For our bad neighbour makes us early stirrers,
Which is both healthful and good husbandry.
Besides, they are our outward consciences
And preachers to us all, admonishing
That we should dress us fairly for our end.
Thus may we gather honey from the weed,
And make a moral of the devil himself.

Enter Erpingham

Good morrow, old Sir Thomas Erpingham:
A good soft pillow for that good white head
Were better than a churlish turf of France.

ERPINGHAM: Not so, my liege; this lodging likes me better,
Since I may say 'Now lie I like a king.'

KING HENRY: 'Tis good for men to love their present pains
Upon example; so the spirit is eased;
And when the mind is quick'ned, out of doubt
The organs, though defunct and dead before,
Break up their drowsy grave and newly move
With casted slough and fresh legerity.
Lend me thy cloak, Sir Thomas. Brothers both,
Commend me to the princes in our camp;
Do my good morrow to them, and anon
Desire them all to my pavilion.

GLOUCESTER: We shall, my liege.

ERPINGHAM: Shall I attend your Grace?

KING HENRY: No, my good knight:
Go with my brothers to my lords of England;
I and my bosom must debate awhile,
And then I would no other company.

ERPINGHAM: The Lord in heaven bless thee, noble Harry!
Exeunt All but the King

KING HENRY: God-a-mercy, old heart! thou speak'st cheerfully.
Enter Pistol

PISTOL: Qui va la?

KING HENRY: A friend.

PISTOL: Discuss unto me: art thou officer,
Or art thou base, common, and popular?

KING HENRY: I am a gentleman of a company.

PISTOL: Trail'st thou the puissant pike?

KING HENRY: Even so. What are you?

PISTOL: As good a gentleman as the Emperor.

KING HENRY: Then you are a better than the King.

PISTOL: The King's a bawcock and a heart of gold,
A lad of life, an imp of fame;
Of parents good, of fist most valiant.
I kiss his dirty shoe, and from heart-string
I love the lovely bully. What is thy name?

KING HENRY: Harry le Roy.

PISTOL: Le Roy! a Cornish name; art thou of Cornish crew?

KING HENRY: No, I am a Welshman.

PISTOL: Know'st thou Fluellen?

KING HENRY: Yes.

PISTOL: Tell him I'll knock his leek about his pate
Upon Saint Davy's day.

KING HENRY: Do not you wear your dagger in your cap that day, lest he knock that about yours.

PISTOL: Art thou his friend?

KING HENRY: And his kinsman too.

PISTOL: The figo for thee, then!

KING HENRY: I thank you; God be with you!

PISTOL: My name is Pistol call'd.
Exit

KING HENRY: It sorts well with your fierceness.
Enter Fluellen and Gower

GOWER: Captain Fluellen!

FLUELLEN: So! in the name of Jesu Christ, speak fewer. It is the greatest admiration in the universal world, when the true and aunchient prerogatifes and laws of the wars is not kept: if you would take the pains but to examine the wars of Pompey the Great, you shall find, I warrant you, that there is no tiddle-taddle nor pibble-pabble in Pompey's camp; I warrant you, you shall find the ceremonies of the wars, and the cares of it, and the forms of it, and the sobriety of it, and the modesty of it, to be otherwise.

GOWER: Why, the enemy is loud; you hear him all night.

FLUELLEN: If the enemy is an ass, and a fool, and a prating coxcomb, is it meet, think you, that we should also, look you, be an ass, and a fool, and a prating coxcomb? In your own conscience, now?

GOWER: I will speak lower.

FLUELLEN: I pray you and beseech you that you will.
Exeunt Gower and Fluellen

KING HENRY: Though it appear a little out of fashion,
There is much care and valour in this Welshman.
Enter Three Soldiers: John Bates, Alexander Court, and Michael Williams

COURT: Brother John Bates, is not that the morning which breaks yonder?

BATES: I think it be; but we have no great cause to desire the approach of day.

WILLIAMS: We see yonder the beginning of the day, but I think we shall never see the end of it. Who goes there?

KING HENRY: A friend.

WILLIAMS: Under what captain serve you?

KING HENRY: Under Sir Thomas Erpingham.

WILLIAMS: A good old commander and a most kind gentleman. I pray you, what thinks he of our estate?

KING HENRY: Even as men wreck'd upon a sand, that look to be wash'd off the next tide.

BATES: He hath not told his thought to the King?

KING HENRY: No; nor it is not meet he should. For though I speak it to you, I think the King is but a man as I am: the violet smells to him as it doth to me; the element shows to him as it doth to me; all his senses have but human conditions; his ceremonies laid by, in his nakedness he appears but a man; and though his affections are higher mounted than ours, yet, when they stoop, they stoop with the like wing. Therefore, when he sees reason of fears, as we do, his fears, out of doubt, be of the same relish as ours are; yet, in reason, no man should possess him with any appearance of fear, lest he, by showing it, should dishearten his army.

BATES: He may show what outward courage he will; but I believe, as cold a night as 'tis, he could wish himself in Thames up to the neck; and so I would he were, and I by him, at all adventures, so we were quit here.

KING HENRY: By my troth, I will speak my conscience of the King: I think he would not wish himself anywhere but where he is.

BATES: Then I would he were here alone; so should he be sure to be ransomed, and a many poor men's lives saved.

KING HENRY: I dare say you love him not so ill to wish him here alone, howsoever you speak this, to feel other men's minds; methinks I could not die anywhere so contented as in the King's company, his cause being just and his quarrel honourable.

WILLIAMS: That's more than we know.

BATES: Ay, or more than we should seek after; for we know enough if we know we are the King's subjects. If his cause be wrong, our obedience to the King wipes the crime of it out of us.

WILLIAMS: But if the cause be not good, the King himself hath a heavy reckoning to make when all those legs and arms and heads, chopp'd off in a battle, shall join together at the latter day and cry all 'We died at such a place'- some swearing, some crying for a surgeon, some upon their wives left poor behind them, some upon the debts they owe, some upon their children rawly left. I am afeard there are few die well that die in a battle; for how can they charitably dispose of anything when blood is their argument? Now, if these men do not die well, it will be a black matter for the King that led them to it; who to disobey were against all proportion of subjection.

KING HENRY: So, if a son that is by his father sent about merchandise do sinfully miscarry upon the sea, the imputation of his wickedness, by your rule, should be imposed upon his father that sent him; or if a servant, under his master's command transporting a sum of money, be assailed by robbers and die in many irreconcil'd iniquities, you may call the business of the master the author of the servant's damnation. But this is not so: the King is not bound to answer the particular endings of his soldiers, the father of his son, nor the master of his servant; for they purpose not their death when they purpose their services. Besides, there is no king, be his cause never so spotless, if it come to the arbitrement of swords, can try it out with all unspotted soldiers: some peradventure have on them the guilt of premeditated and contrived murder; some, of beguiling virgins with the broken seals of perjury; some, making the wars their bulwark, that have before gored the gentle bosom of peace with pillage and robbery. Now, if these men have defeated the law and outrun native punishment, though they can outstrip men they have no wings to fly from God: war is His beadle, war is His vengeance; so that here men are punish'd for before-breach of the King's laws in now the King's quarrel. Where they feared the death they have borne life away; and where they would be safe they perish. Then if they die unprovided, no more is the King guilty of their damnation than he was before guilty of those impieties for the which they are now visited. Every subject's duty is the King's; but every subject's soul is his own. Therefore should every soldier in the wars do as every sick man in his bed- wash every mote out of his conscience; and dying so, death is to him advantage; or not dying, the time was blessedly lost wherein such preparation was gained; and in him that escapes it were not sin to think that, making God so free an offer, He let him outlive that day to see His greatness, and to teach others how they should prepare.

WILLIAMS: 'Tis certain, every man that dies ill, the ill upon his own head- the King is not to answer for it.

BATES: I do not desire he should answer for me, and yet I determine to fight lustily for him.

KING HENRY: I myself heard the King say he would not be ransom'd.

WILLIAMS: Ay, he said so, to make us fight cheerfully; but when our throats are cut he may be ransom'd, and we ne'er the wiser.

KING HENRY: If I live to see it, I will never trust his word after.

WILLIAMS: You pay him then! That's a perilous shot out of an elder-gun, that a poor and a private displeasure can do against a monarch! You may as well go about to turn the sun to ice with fanning in his face with a peacock's feather. You'll never trust his word after! Come, 'tis a foolish saying.

KING HENRY: Your reproof is something too round; I should be angry with you, if the time were convenient.

WILLIAMS: Let it be a quarrel between us if you live.

KING HENRY: I embrace it.

WILLIAMS: How shall I know thee again?

KING HENRY: Give me any gage of thine, and I will wear it in my bonnet; then if ever thou dar'st acknowledge it, I will make it my quarrel.

WILLIAMS: Here's my glove; give me another of thine.

KING HENRY: There.

WILLIAMS: This will I also wear in my cap; if ever thou come to me and say, after to-morrow, 'This is my glove,' by this hand I will take thee a box on the ear.

KING HENRY: If ever I live to see it, I will challenge it.

WILLIAMS: Thou dar'st as well be hang'd.

KING HENRY: Well, I will do it, though I take thee in the King's company.

WILLIAMS: Keep thy word. Fare thee well.

BATES: Be friends, you English fools, be friends; we have
French quarrels enow, if you could tell how to reckon.

KING HENRY: Indeed, the French may lay twenty French crowns to one they will beat us, for they bear them on their shoulders; but it is no English treason to cut French crowns, and to-morrow the
King himself will be a clipper.
Exeunt Soldiers
Upon the King! Let us our lives, our souls,
Our debts, our careful wives,
Our children, and our sins, lay on the King!
We must bear all. O hard condition,
Twin-born with greatness, subject to the breath
Of every fool, whose sense no more can feel
But his own wringing! What infinite heart's ease
Must kings neglect that private men enjoy!
And what have kings that privates have not too,
Save ceremony- save general ceremony?
And what art thou, thou idol Ceremony?
What kind of god art thou, that suffer'st more
Of mortal griefs than do thy worshippers?
What are thy rents? What are thy comings-in?
O Ceremony, show me but thy worth!
What is thy soul of adoration?
Art thou aught else but place, degree, and form,
Creating awe and fear in other men?
Wherein thou art less happy being fear'd
Than they in fearing.
What drink'st thou oft, instead of homage sweet,
But poison'd flattery? O, be sick, great greatness,
And bid thy ceremony give thee cure!
Thinks thou the fiery fever will go out
With titles blown from adulation?

Will it give place to flexure and low bending?
Canst thou, when thou command'st the beggar's knee,
Command the health of it? No, thou proud dream,
That play'st so subtly with a king's repose.
I am a king that find thee; and I know
'Tis not the balm, the sceptre, and the ball,
The sword, the mace, the crown imperial,
The intertissued robe of gold and pearl,
The farced tide running fore the king,
The throne he sits on, nor the tide of pomp
That beats upon the high shore of this world-
No, not all these, thrice gorgeous ceremony,
Not all these, laid in bed majestical,
Can sleep so soundly as the wretched slave
Who, with a body fill'd and vacant mind,
Gets him to rest, cramm'd with distressful bread;
Never sees horrid night, the child of hell;
But, like a lackey, from the rise to set
Sweats in the eye of Pheebus, and all night
Sleeps in Elysium; next day, after dawn,
Doth rise and help Hyperion to his horse;
And follows so the ever-running year
With profitable labour, to his grave.
And but for ceremony, such a wretch,
Winding up days with toil and nights with sleep,
Had the fore-hand and vantage of a king.
The slave, a member of the country's peace,
Enjoys it; but in gross brain little wots
What watch the king keeps to maintain the peace
Whose hours the peasant best advantages.
Enter Erpingham

ERPINGHAM: My lord, your nobles, jealous of your absence,
Seek through your camp to find you.

KING: Good old knight,
Collect them all together at my tent:

I'll be before thee.

ERPINGHAM: I shall do't, my lord.
Exit

KING: O God of battles, steel my soldiers' hearts,
Possess them not with fear! Take from them now
The sense of reck'ning, if th' opposed numbers
Pluck their hearts from them! Not to-day, O Lord,
O, not to-day, think not upon the fault
My father made in compassing the crown!
I Richard's body have interred new,
And on it have bestowed more contrite tears
Than from it issued forced drops of blood;
Five hundred poor I have in yearly pay,
Who twice a day their wither'd hands hold up
Toward heaven, to pardon blood; and I have built
Two chantries, where the sad and solemn priests
Sing still for Richard's soul. More will I do;
Though all that I can do is nothing worth,
Since that my penitence comes after all,
Imploring pardon.
Enter Gloucester

GLOUCESTER: My liege!

KING HENRY: My brother Gloucester's voice? Ay;
I know thy errand, I will go with thee;
The day, my friends, and all things, stay for me.
Exeunt

ACT IV. SCENE II. The French Camp

Enter the Dauphin, Orleans, Rambures, and Others

ORLEANS: The sun doth gild our armour; up, my lords!

DAUPHIN: Montez a cheval! My horse! Varlet, laquais! Ha!

ORLEANS: O brave spirit!

DAUPHIN: Via! Les eaux et la terre-

ORLEANS: Rien puis? L'air et le feu.

DAUPHIN: Ciel! cousin Orleans.
Enter Constable
Now, my Lord Constable!

CONSTABLE: Hark how our steeds for present service neigh!

DAUPHIN: Mount them, and make incision in their hides,
That their hot blood may spin in English eyes,
And dout them with superfluous courage, ha!

RAMBURES: What, will you have them weep our horses' blood?
How shall we then behold their natural tears?
Enter a Messenger

MESSENGER: The English are embattl'd, you French peers.

CONSTABLE: To horse, you gallant Princes! straight to horse!
Do but behold yon poor and starved band,
And your fair show shall suck away their souls,
Leaving them but the shales and husks of men.
There is not work enough for all our hands;
Scarce blood enough in all their sickly veins
To give each naked curtle-axe a stain
That our French gallants shall to-day draw out,
And sheathe for lack of sport. Let us but blow on them,
The vapour of our valour will o'erturn them.
'Tis positive 'gainst all exceptions, lords,
That our superfluous lackeys and our peasants-
Who in unnecessary action swarm
About our squares of battle- were enow
To purge this field of, such a hilding foe;

Though we upon this mountain's basis by
Took stand for idle speculation-
But that our honours must not. What's to say?
A very little little let us do,
And all is done. Then let the trumpets sound
The tucket sonance and the note to mount;
For our approach shall so much dare the field
That England shall couch down in fear and yield.
Enter Grandpre

GRANDPRE: Why do you stay so long, my lords of France?
Yond island carrions, desperate of their bones,
Ill-favouredly become the morning field;
Their ragged curtains poorly are let loose,
And our air shakes them passing scornfully;
Big Mars seems bankrupt in their beggar'd host,
And faintly through a rusty beaver peeps.
The horsemen sit like fixed candlesticks
With torch-staves in their hand; and their poor jades
Lob down their heads, dropping the hides and hips,
The gum down-roping from their pale-dead eyes,
And in their pale dull mouths the gimmal'd bit
Lies foul with chaw'd grass, still and motionless;
And their executors, the knavish crows,
Fly o'er them, all impatient for their hour.
Description cannot suit itself in words
To demonstrate the life of such a battle
In life so lifeless as it shows itself.

CONSTABLE: They have said their prayers and they stay for death.

DAUPHIN: Shall we go send them dinners and fresh suits,
And give their fasting horses provender,
And after fight with them?

CONSTABLE: I stay but for my guidon. To the field!
I will the banner from a trumpet take,

And use it for my haste. Come, come, away!
The sun is high, and we outwear the day.
Exeunt

ACT IV. SCENE III. The English Camp

Enter Gloucester, Bedford, Exeter, Erpingham, with All His Host; Salisbury and Westmoreland

GLOUCESTER: Where is the King?

BEDFORD: The King himself is rode to view their battle.

WESTMORELAND: Of fighting men they have full three-score thousand.

EXETER: There's five to one; besides, they all are fresh.

SALISBURY: God's arm strike with us! 'tis a fearful odds.
God bye you, Princes all; I'll to my charge.
If we no more meet till we meet in heaven,
Then joyfully, my noble Lord of Bedford,
My dear Lord Gloucester, and my good Lord Exeter,
And my kind kinsman- warriors all, adieu!

BEDFORD: Farewell, good Salisbury; and good luck go with thee!

EXETER: Farewell, kind lord. Fight valiantly to-day;
And yet I do thee wrong to mind thee of it,
For thou art fram'd of the firm truth of valour.
Exit Salisbury

BEDFORD: He is as full of valour as of kindness;
Princely in both.
Enter the King

WESTMORELAND: O that we now had here
But one ten thousand of those men in England
That do no work to-day!

KING: What's he that wishes so?
My cousin Westmoreland? No, my fair cousin;
If we are mark'd to die, we are enow
To do our country loss; and if to live,
The fewer men, the greater share of honour.
God's will! I pray thee, wish not one man more.
By Jove, I am not covetous for gold,
Nor care I who doth feed upon my cost;
It yearns me not if men my garments wear;
Such outward things dwell not in my desires.
But if it be a sin to covet honour,
I am the most offending soul alive.
No, faith, my coz, wish not a man from England.
God's peace! I would not lose so great an honour
As one man more methinks would share from me
For the best hope I have. O, do not wish one more!
Rather proclaim it, Westmoreland, through my host,
That he which hath no stomach to this fight,
Let him depart; his passport shall be made,
And crowns for convoy put into his purse;
We would not die in that man's company
That fears his fellowship to die with us.
This day is call'd the feast of Crispian.
He that outlives this day, and comes safe home,
Will stand a tip-toe when this day is nam'd,
And rouse him at the name of Crispian.
He that shall live this day, and see old age,
Will yearly on the vigil feast his neighbours,
And say 'To-morrow is Saint Crispian.'
Then will he strip his sleeve and show his scars,
And say 'These wounds I had on Crispian's day.'
Old men forget; yet all shall be forgot,
But he'll remember, with advantages,
What feats he did that day. Then shall our names,
Familiar in his mouth as household words-
Harry the King, Bedford and Exeter,
Warwick and Talbot, Salisbury and Gloucester-

Be in their flowing cups freshly rememb'red.
This story shall the good man teach his son;
And Crispin Crispian shall ne'er go by,
From this day to the ending of the world,
But we in it shall be remembered-
We few, we happy few, we band of brothers;
For he to-day that sheds his blood with me
Shall be my brother; be he ne'er so vile,
This day shall gentle his condition;
And gentlemen in England now-a-bed
Shall think themselves accurs'd they were not here,
And hold their manhoods cheap whiles any speaks
That fought with us upon Saint Crispin's day.
Re-enter Salisbury

SALISBURY: My sovereign lord, bestow yourself with speed:
The French are bravely in their battles set,
And will with all expedience charge on us.

KING HENRY: All things are ready, if our minds be so.

WESTMORELAND: Perish the man whose mind is backward now!

KING HENRY: Thou dost not wish more help from England, coz?

WESTMORELAND: God's will, my liege! would you and I alone,
Without more help, could fight this royal battle!

KING HENRY: Why, now thou hast unwish'd five thousand men;
Which likes me better than to wish us one.
You know your places. God be with you all!
Tucket. Enter Montjoy

MONTJOY: Once more I come to know of thee, King Harry,
If for thy ransom thou wilt now compound,
Before thy most assured overthrow;
For certainly thou art so near the gulf

Thou needs must be englutted. Besides, in mercy,
The constable desires thee thou wilt mind
Thy followers of repentance, that their souls
May make a peaceful and a sweet retire
From off these fields, where, wretches, their poor bodies
Must lie and fester.

KING HENRY: Who hath sent thee now?

MONTJOY: The Constable of France.

KING HENRY: I pray thee bear my former answer back:
Bid them achieve me, and then sell my bones.
Good God! why should they mock poor fellows thus?
The man that once did sell the lion's skin
While the beast liv'd was kill'd with hunting him.
A many of our bodies shall no doubt
Find native graves; upon the which, I trust,
Shall witness live in brass of this day's work.
And those that leave their valiant bones in France,
Dying like men, though buried in your dunghills,
They shall be fam'd; for there the sun shall greet them
And draw their honours reeking up to heaven,
Leaving their earthly parts to choke your clime,
The smell whereof shall breed a plague in France.
Mark then abounding valour in our English,
That, being dead, like to the bullet's grazing
Break out into a second course of mischief,
Killing in relapse of mortality.
Let me speak proudly: tell the Constable
We are but warriors for the working-day;
Our gayness and our gilt are all besmirch'd
With rainy marching in the painful field;
There's not a piece of feather in our host-
Good argument, I hope, we will not fly-
And time hath worn us into slovenry.
But, by the mass, our hearts are in the trim;

And my poor soldiers tell me yet ere night
They'll be in fresher robes, or they will pluck
The gay new coats o'er the French soldiers' heads
And turn them out of service. If they do this-
As, if God please, they shall- my ransom then
Will soon be levied. Herald, save thou thy labour;
Come thou no more for ransom, gentle herald;
They shall have none, I swear, but these my joints;
Which if they have, as I will leave 'em them,
Shall yield them little, tell the Constable.

MONTJOY: I shall, King Harry. And so fare thee well:
Thou never shalt hear herald any more.
Exit

KING HENRY: I fear thou wilt once more come again for a ransom.
Enter the Duke of York

YORK: My lord, most humbly on my knee I beg
The leading of the vaward.

KING HENRY: Take it, brave York. Now, soldiers, march away;
And how thou pleasest, God, dispose the day!
Exeunt

ACT IV. SCENE IV. The Field of Battle

Alarum. Excursions. Enter French Soldier, Pistol, and Boy

PISTOL: Yield, cur!

FRENCH SOLDIER: Je pense que vous etes le gentilhomme de bonne qualite.

PISTOL: Cality! Calen o custure me! Art thou a gentleman?
What is thy name? Discuss.

FRENCH SOLDIER: O Seigneur Dieu!

PISTOL: O, Signieur Dew should be a gentleman.
Perpend my words, O Signieur Dew, and mark:
O Signieur Dew, thou diest on point of fox,
Except, O Signieur, thou do give to me
Egregious ransom.

FRENCH SOLDIER: O, prenez misericorde; ayez pitie de moi!

PISTOL: Moy shall not serve; I will have forty moys;
Or I will fetch thy rim out at thy throat
In drops of crimson blood.

FRENCH SOLDIER: Est-il impossible d'echapper la force de ton bras?

PISTOL: Brass, cur?
Thou damned and luxurious mountain-goat,
Offer'st me brass?

FRENCH SOLDIER: O, pardonnez-moi!

PISTOL: Say'st thou me so? Is that a ton of moys?
Come hither, boy; ask me this slave in French
What is his name.

BOY: Ecoutez: comment etes-vous appele?

FRENCH SOLDIER: Monsieur le Fer.

BOY: He says his name is Master Fer.

PISTOL: Master Fer! I'll fer him, and firk him, and ferret him-discuss the same in French unto him.

BOY: I do not know the French for fer, and ferret, and firk.

PISTOL: Bid him prepare; for I will cut his throat.

FRENCH SOLDIER: Que dit-il, monsieur?

BOY: Il me commande a vous dire que vous faites vous pret; car ce soldat ici est dispose tout a cette heure de couper votre gorge.

PISTOL: Owy, cuppele gorge, permafoy!
Peasant, unless thou give me crowns, brave crowns;
Or mangled shalt thou be by this my sword.

FRENCH SOLDIER: O, je vous supplie, pour l'amour de Dieu, me pardonner! Je suis gentilhomme de bonne maison. Gardez ma vie, et je vous donnerai deux cents ecus.

PISTOL: What are his words?

BOY: He prays you to save his life; he is a gentleman of a good house, and for his ransom he will give you two hundred crowns.

PISTOL: Tell him my fury shall abate, and I
The crowns will take.

FRENCH SOLDIER: Petit monsieur, que dit-il?

BOY: Encore qu'il est contre son jurement de pardonner aucun prisonnier, neamnoins, pour les ecus que vous l'avez promis, il est content a vous donner la liberte, le franchisement.

FRENCH SOLDIER: Sur mes genoux je vous donne mille remercimens; et je m'estime heureux que je suis tombe entre les mains d'un chevalier, je pense, le plus brave, vaillant, et tres distingue seigneur d'Angleterre.

PISTOL: Expound unto me, boy.

BOY: He gives you, upon his knees, a thousand thanks; and he esteems himself happy that he hath fall'n into the hands of one- as he thinks- the most brave, valorous, and thrice-worthy signieur of England.

PISTOL: As I suck blood, I will some mercy show. Follow me.
Exit

BOY: Suivez-vous le grand capitaine.
Exit French Soldier
I did never know so full a voice issue from so empty a heart; but the saying is true- the empty vessel makes the greatest sound. Bardolph and Nym had ten times more valour than this roaring devil i' th' old play, that every one may pare his nails with a wooden dagger; and they are both hang'd; and so would this be, if he durst steal anything adventurously. I must stay with the lackeys, with the luggage of our camp. The French might have a good prey of us, if he knew of it; for there is none to guard it but boys.
Exit

ACT IV. SCENE V. Another Part of the Field of Battle
Enter Constable, Orleans, Bourbon, Dauphin, and Rambures

CONSTABLE: O diable!

ORLEANS: O Seigneur! le jour est perdu, tout est perdu!

DAUPHIN: Mort Dieu, ma vie! all is confounded, all!
Reproach and everlasting shame
Sits mocking in our plumes. *A Short Alarum*
O mechante fortune! Do not run away.

CONSTABLE: Why, an our ranks are broke.

DAUPHIN: O perdurable shame! Let's stab ourselves.
Be these the wretches that we play'd at dice for?

ORLEANS: Is this the king we sent to for his ransom?

BOURBON: Shame, and eternal shame, nothing but shame!
Let us die in honour: once more back again;
And he that will not follow Bourbon now,
Let him go hence and, with his cap in hand

Like a base pander, hold the chamber-door
Whilst by a slave, no gender than my dog,
His fairest daughter is contaminated.

CONSTABLE: Disorder, that hath spoil'd us, friend us now!
Let us on heaps go offer up our lives.

ORLEANS: We are enow yet living in the field
To smother up the English in our throngs,
If any order might be thought upon.

BOURBON: The devil take order now! I'll to the throng.
Let life be short, else shame will be too long.
Exeunt

ACT IV. SCENE VI. Another Part of the Field

Alarum. Enter the King and His Train, with Prisoners; Exeter, and Others

KING HENRY: Well have we done, thrice-valiant countrymen;
But all's not done- yet keep the French the field.

EXETER: The Duke of York commends him to your Majesty.

KING HENRY: Lives he, good uncle? Thrice within this hour
I saw him down; thrice up again, and fighting;
From helmet to the spur all blood he was.

EXETER: In which array, brave soldier, doth he lie
Larding the plain; and by his bloody side,
Yoke-fellow to his honour-owing wounds,
The noble Earl of Suffolk also lies.
Suffolk first died; and York, all haggled over,
Comes to him, where in gore he lay insteeped,
And takes him by the beard, kisses the gashes
That bloodily did yawn upon his face,
He cries aloud 'Tarry, my cousin Suffolk.
My soul shall thine keep company to heaven;

Tarry, sweet soul, for mine, then fly abreast;
As in this glorious and well-foughten field
We kept together in our chivalry.'
Upon these words I came and cheer'd him up;
He smil'd me in the face, raught me his hand,
And, with a feeble grip, says 'Dear my lord,
Commend my service to my sovereign.'
So did he turn, and over Suffolk's neck
He threw his wounded arm and kiss'd his lips;
And so, espous'd to death, with blood he seal'd
A testament of noble-ending love.
The pretty and sweet manner of it forc'd
Those waters from me which I would have stopp'd;
But I had not so much of man in me,
And all my mother came into mine eyes
And gave me up to tears.

KING HENRY: I blame you not;
For, hearing this, I must perforce compound
With mistful eyes, or they will issue too. *Alarum*
But hark! what new alarum is this same?
The French have reinforc'd their scatter'd men.
Then every soldier kill his prisoners;
Give the word through.
Exeunt

ACT IV. SCENE VII. Another Part of the Field

Enter Fluellen and Gower

FLUELLEN: Kill the poys and the luggage! 'Tis expressly against the law of arms; 'tis as arrant a piece of knavery, mark you now, as can be offert; in your conscience, now, is it not?

GOWER: 'Tis certain there's not a boy left alive; and the cowardly rascals that ran from the battle ha' done this slaughter; besides, they have burned and carried away all that was in the King's tent; wherefore the King most worthily hath caus'd every soldier to cut his prisoner's throat. O, 'tis a gallant King!

FLUELLEN: Ay, he was porn at Monmouth, Captain Gower. What call you the town's name where Alexander the Pig was born?

GOWER: Alexander the Great.

FLUELLEN: Why, I pray you, is not 'pig' great? The pig, or great, or the mighty, or the huge, or the magnanimous, are all one reckonings, save the phrase is a little variations.

GOWER: I think Alexander the Great was born in Macedon; his father was called Philip of Macedon, as I take it.

FLUELLEN: I think it is in Macedon where Alexander is porn. I tell you, Captain, if you look in the maps of the 'orld, I warrant you sall find, in the comparisons between Macedon and Monmouth, that the situations, look you, is both alike. There is a river in Macedon; and there is also moreover a river at Monmouth; it is call'd Wye at Monmouth, but it is out of my prains what is the name of the other river; but 'tis all one, 'tis alike as my fingers is to my fingers, and there is salmons in both. If you mark Alexander's life well, Harry of Monmouth's life is come after it indifferent well; for there is figures in all things. Alexander- God knows, and you know- in his rages, and his furies, and his wraths, and his cholers, and his moods, and his displeasures, and his indignations, and also being a little intoxicates in his prains, did, in his ales and his angers, look you, kill his best friend, Cleitus.

GOWER: Our king is not like him in that: he never kill'd any of his friends.

FLUELLEN: It is not well done, mark you now, to take the tales out of my mouth ere it is made and finished. I speak but in the figures and comparisons of it; as Alexander kill'd his friend Cleitus, being in his ales and his cups, so also Harry Monmouth, being in his right wits and his good judgments, turn'd away the fat knight with the great belly doublet; he was full of jests, and gipes, and knaveries, and mocks; I have forgot his name.

GOWER: Sir John Falstaff.

FLUELLEN: That is he. I'll tell you there is good men porn at Monmouth.

GOWER: Here comes his Majesty.

Alarum. Enter the King, Warwick, Gloucester, Exeter, and Others, with Prisoners. Flourish

KING HENRY: I was not angry since I came to France
Until this instant. Take a trumpet, herald,
Ride thou unto the horsemen on yond hill;
If they will fight with us, bid them come down
Or void the field; they do offend our sight.
If they'll do neither, we will come to them
And make them skirr away as swift as stones
Enforced from the old Assyrian slings;
Besides, we'll cut the throats of those we have,
And not a man of them that we shall take
Shall taste our mercy. Go and tell them so.

Enter Montjoy

EXETER: Here comes the herald of the French, my liege.

GLOUCESTER: His eyes are humbler than they us'd to be.

KING HENRY: How now! What means this, herald? know'st thou not
That I have fin'd these bones of mine for ransom?
Com'st thou again for ransom?

MONTJOY: No, great King;
I come to thee for charitable licence,
That we may wander o'er this bloody field
To book our dead, and then to bury them;
To sort our nobles from our common men;
For many of our princes- woe the while!-
Lie drown'd and soak'd in mercenary blood;
So do our vulgar drench their peasant limbs

In blood of princes; and their wounded steeds
Fret fetlock deep in gore, and with wild rage
Yerk out their armed heels at their dead masters,
Killing them twice. O, give us leave, great King,
To view the field in safety, and dispose
Of their dead bodies!

KING HENRY: I tell thee truly, herald,
I know not if the day be ours or no;
For yet a many of your horsemen peer
And gallop o'er the field.

MONTJOY: The day is yours.

KING HENRY: Praised be God, and not our strength, for it!
What is this castle call'd that stands hard by?

MONTJOY: They call it Agincourt.

KING HENRY: Then call we this the field of Agincourt,
Fought on the day of Crispin Crispianus.

FLUELLEN: Your grandfather of famous memory, an't please your Majesty, and your great-uncle Edward the Plack Prince of Wales, as I have read in the chronicles, fought a most prave pattle here in France.

KING HENRY: They did, Fluellen.

FLUELLEN: Your Majesty says very true; if your Majesties is rememb'red of it, the Welshmen did good service in garden where leeks did grow, wearing leeks in their Monmouth caps; which your Majesty know to this hour is an honourable badge of the service; and I do believe your Majesty takes no scorn to wear the leek upon Saint Tavy's day.

KING HENRY: I wear it for a memorable honour;
For I am Welsh, you know, good countryman.

FLUELLEN: All the water in Wye cannot wash your Majesty's Welsh plood out of your pody, I can tell you that. Got pless it and preserve it as long as it pleases his Grace and his Majesty too!

KING HENRY: Thanks, good my countryman.

FLUELLEN: By Jeshu, I am your Majesty's countryman, care not who know it; I will confess it to all the 'orld: I need not be asham'd of your Majesty, praised be Got, so long as your Majesty is an honest man.

Enter Williams

KING HENRY: God keep me so! Our heralds go with him:
Bring me just notice of the numbers dead
On both our parts. Call yonder fellow hither.

Exeunt Heralds with Montjoy

EXETER: Soldier, you must come to the King.

KING HENRY: Soldier, why wear'st thou that glove in thy cap?

WILLIAMS: An't please your Majesty, 'tis the gage of one that I should fight withal, if he be alive.

KING HENRY: An Englishman?

WILLIAMS: An't please your Majesty, a rascal that swagger'd with me last night; who, if 'a live and ever dare to challenge this glove, I have sworn to take him a box o' th' ear; or if I can see my glove in his cap- which he swore, as he was a soldier, he would wear if alive- I will strike it out soundly.

KING HENRY: What think you, Captain Fluellen, is it fit this soldier keep his oath?

FLUELLEN: He is a craven and a villain else, an't please your Majesty, in my conscience.

KING HENRY: It may be his enemy is a gentlemen of great sort, quite from the answer of his degree.

FLUELLEN: Though he be as good a gentleman as the Devil is, as Lucifier and Belzebub himself, it is necessary, look your Grace, that he keep his vow and his oath; if he be perjur'd, see you now, his reputation is as arrant a villain and a Jacksauce as ever his black shoe trod upon God's ground and his earth, in my conscience, la.

KING HENRY: Then keep thy vow, sirrah, when thou meet'st the fellow.

WILLIAMS: So I Will, my liege, as I live.

KING HENRY: Who serv'st thou under?

WILLIAMS: Under Captain Gower, my liege.

FLUELLEN: Gower is a good captain, and is good knowledge and literatured in the wars.

KING HENRY: Call him hither to me, soldier.

WILLIAMS: I will, my liege.
Exit

KING HENRY: Here, Fluellen; wear thou this favour for me, and stick it in thy cap; when Alencon and myself were down together, I pluck'd this glove from his helm. If any man challenge this, he is a friend to Alencon and an enemy to our person; if thou encounter any such, apprehend him, an thou dost me love.

FLUELLEN: Your Grace does me as great honours as can be desir'd in the hearts of his subjects. I would fain see the man that has but two legs that shall find himself aggrief'd at this glove, that is all; but I would fain see it once, an please God of his grace that I might see.

KING HENRY: Know'st thou Gower?

FLUELLEN: He is my dear friend, an please you.

KING HENRY: Pray thee, go seek him, and bring him to my tent.

FLUELLEN: I will fetch him.
Exit

KING HENRY: My Lord of Warwick and my brother Gloucester,
Follow Fluellen closely at the heels;
The glove which I have given him for a favour
May haply purchase him a box o' th' ear.
It is the soldier's: I, by bargain, should
Wear it myself. Follow, good cousin Warwick;
If that the soldier strike him, as I judge
By his blunt bearing he will keep his word,
Some sudden mischief may arise of it;
For I do know Fluellen valiant,
And touch'd with choler, hot as gunpowder,
And quickly will return an injury;
Follow, and see there be no harm between them.
Go you with me, uncle of Exeter.
Exeunt

ACT IV. SCENE VIII. Before King Henry's Pavilion

Enter Gower and Williams

WILLIAMS: I warrant it is to knight you, Captain.
Enter Fluellen

FLUELLEN: God's will and his pleasure, Captain, I beseech you now, come apace to the King: there is more good toward you peradventure than is in your knowledge to dream of.

WILLIAMS: Sir, know you this glove?

FLUELLEN: Know the glove? I know the glove is a glove.

WILLIAMS: I know this; and thus I challenge it. *Strikes Him*

FLUELLEN: 'Sblood, an arrant traitor as any's in the universal world, or in France, or in England!

GOWER: How now, sir! you villain!

WILLIAMS: Do you think I'll be forsworn?

FLUELLEN: Stand away, Captain Gower; I will give treason his payment into plows, I warrant you.

WILLIAMS: I am no traitor.

FLUELLEN: That's a lie in thy throat. I charge you in his Majesty's name, apprehend him: he's a friend of the Duke Alencon's.
Enter Warwick and Gloucester

WARWICK: How now! how now! what's the matter?

FLUELLEN: My Lord of Warwick, here is- praised be God for it!- a most contagious treason come to light, look you, as you shall desire in a summer's day. Here is his Majesty.
Enter the King and Exeter

KING HENRY: How now! what's the matter?

FLUELLEN: My liege, here is a villain and a traitor, that, look your Grace, has struck the glove which your Majesty is take out of the helmet of Alencon.

WILLIAMS: My liege, this was my glove: here is the fellow of it; and he that I gave it to in change promis'd to wear it in his cap; I promis'd to strike him if he did; I met this man with my glove in his cap, and I have been as good as my word.

FLUELLEN: Your Majesty hear now, saving your Majesty's manhood, what an arrant, rascally, beggarly, lousy knave it is; I hope your Majesty is pear me testimony and witness, and will avouchment, that this is the glove of Alencon that your Majesty is give me; in your conscience, now.

KING HENRY: Give me thy glove, soldier; look, here is the fellow of it.
'Twas I, indeed, thou promised'st to strike,
And thou hast given me most bitter terms.

FLUELLEN: An please your Majesty, let his neck answer for it, if there is any martial law in the world.

KING HENRY: How canst thou make me satisfaction?

WILLIAMS: All offences, my lord, come from the heart; never came any from mine that might offend your Majesty.

KING HENRY: It was ourself thou didst abuse.

WILLIAMS: Your Majesty came not like yourself: you appear'd to me but as a common man; witness the night, your garments, your lowliness; and what your Highness suffer'd under that shape I beseech you take it for your own fault, and not mine; for had you been as I took you for, I made no offence; therefore, I beseech your Highness pardon me.

KING HENRY: Here, uncle Exeter, fill this glove with crowns,
And give it to this fellow. Keep it, fellow;
And wear it for an honour in thy cap
Till I do challenge it. Give him the crowns;
And, Captain, you must needs be friends with him.

FLUELLEN: By this day and this light, the fellow has mettle enough in his belly: hold, there is twelve pence for you; and I pray you to serve God, and keep you out of prawls, and prabbles, and quarrels, and dissensions, and, I warrant you, it is the better for you.

WILLIAMS: I will none of your money.

FLUELLEN: It is with a good will; I can tell you it will serve you to mend your shoes. Come, wherefore should you be so pashful? Your shoes is not so good. 'Tis a good silling, I warrant you, or I will change it.
Enter an English Herald

KING HENRY: Now, herald, are the dead numb'red?

HERALD: Here is the number of the slaught'red French.
Gives a Paper

KING HENRY: What prisoners of good sort are taken, uncle?

EXETER: Charles Duke of Orleans, nephew to the King;
John Duke of Bourbon, and Lord Bouciqualt;
Of other lords and barons, knights and squires,
Full fifteen hundred, besides common men.

KING HENRY: This note doth tell me of ten thousand French
That in the field lie slain; of princes in this number,
And nobles bearing banners, there lie dead
One hundred twenty-six; added to these,
Of knights, esquires, and gallant gentlemen,
Eight thousand and four hundred; of the which
Five hundred were but yesterday dubb'd knights.
So that, in these ten thousand they have lost,
There are but sixteen hundred mercenaries;
The rest are princes, barons, lords, knights, squires,
And gentlemen of blood and quality.
The names of those their nobles that lie dead:
Charles Delabreth, High Constable of France;
Jaques of Chatillon, Admiral of France;
The master of the cross-bows, Lord Rambures;
Great Master of France, the brave Sir Guichard Dolphin;
John Duke of Alencon; Antony Duke of Brabant,
The brother to the Duke of Burgundy;
And Edward Duke of Bar. Of lusty earls,
Grandpre and Roussi, Fauconbridge and Foix,

Beaumont and Marle, Vaudemont and Lestrake.
Here was a royal fellowship of death!
Where is the number of our English dead?
Herald Presents Another Paper
Edward the Duke of York, the Earl of Suffolk,
Sir Richard Kikely, Davy Gam, Esquire;
None else of name; and of all other men
But five and twenty. O God, thy arm was here!
And not to us, but to thy arm alone,
Ascribe we all. When, without stratagem,
But in plain shock and even play of battle,
Was ever known so great and little los
On one part and on th' other? Take it, God,
For it is none but thine.

EXETER: 'Tis wonderful!

KING HENRY: Come, go we in procession to the village;
And be it death proclaimed through our host
To boast of this or take that praise from God
Which is his only.

FLUELLEN: Is it not lawful, an please your Majesty, to tell how many is kill'd?

KING HENRY: Yes, Captain; but with this acknowledgment,
That God fought for us.

FLUELLEN: Yes, my conscience, he did us great good.

KING HENRY: Do we all holy rites:
Let there be sung 'Non nobis' and 'Te Deum';
The dead with charity enclos'd in clay-
And then to Calais; and to England then;
Where ne'er from France arriv'd more happy men.
Exeunt

ACT V. PROLOGUE. Enter Chorus

CHORUS: Vouchsafe to those that have not read the story
That I may prompt them; and of such as have,
I humbly pray them to admit th' excuse
Of time, of numbers, and due course of things,
Which cannot in their huge and proper life
Be here presented. Now we bear the King
Toward Calais. Grant him there. There seen,
Heave him away upon your winged thoughts
Athwart the sea. Behold, the English beach
Pales in the flood with men, with wives, and boys,
Whose shouts and claps out-voice the deep-mouth'd sea,
Which, like a mighty whiffler, fore the King
Seems to prepare his way. So let him land,
And solemnly see him set on to London.
So swift a pace hath thought that even now
You may imagine him upon Blackheath;
Where that his lords desire him to have borne
His bruised helmet and his bended sword
Before him through the city. He forbids it,
Being free from vainness and self-glorious pride;
Giving full trophy, signal, and ostent,
Quite from himself to God. But now behold
In the quick forge and working-house of thought,
How London doth pour out her citizens!
The mayor and all his brethren in best sort-
Like to the senators of th' antique Rome,
With the plebeians swarming at their heels-
Go forth and fetch their conqu'ring Caesar in;
As, by a lower but loving likelihood,
Were now the General of our gracious Empress-
As in good time he may- from Ireland coming,
Bringing rebellion broached on his sword,
How many would the peaceful city quit
To welcome him! Much more, and much more cause,
Did they this Harry. Now in London place him-

As yet the lamentation of the French
Invites the King of England's stay at home;
The Emperor's coming in behalf of France
To order peace between them; and omit
All the occurrences, whatever chanc'd,
Till Harry's back-return again to France.
There must we bring him; and myself have play'd
The interim, by rememb'ring you 'tis past.
Then brook abridgment; and your eyes advance,
After your thoughts, straight back again to France.
Exit

ACT V. SCENE I. France. The English Camp

Enter Fluellen and Gower

GOWER: Nay, that's right; but why wear you your leek to-day? Saint Davy's day is past.

FLUELLEN: There is occasions and causes why and wherefore in all things. I will tell you, ass my friend, Captain Gower: the rascally, scald, beggarly, lousy, pragging knave, Pistol- which you and yourself and all the world know to be no petter than a fellow, look you now, of no merits- he is come to me, and prings me pread and salt yesterday, look you, and bid me eat my leek; it was in a place where I could not breed no contendon with him; but I will be so bold as to wear it in my cap till I see him once again, and then I will tell him a little piece of my desires.
Enter Pistol

GOWER: Why, here he comes, swelling like a turkey-cock.

FLUELLEN: 'Tis no matter for his swellings nor his turkey-cocks. God pless you, Aunchient Pistol! you scurvy, lousy knave, God pless you!

PISTOL: Ha! art thou bedlam? Dost thou thirst, base Troyan,
To have me fold up Parca's fatal web?
Hence! I am qualmish at the smell of leek.

FLUELLEN: I peseech you heartily, scurvy, lousy knave, at my desires, and my requests, and my petitions, to eat, look you, this leek; because, look you, you do not love it, nor your affections, and your appetites, and your digestions, does not agree with it, I would desire you to eat it.

PISTOL: Not for Cadwallader and all his goats.

FLUELLEN: There is one goat for you. *Strikes Him* Will you be so good, scald knave, as eat it?

PISTOL: Base Troyan, thou shalt die.

FLUELLEN: You say very true, scald knave- when God's will is. I will desire you to live in the meantime, and eat your victuals; come, there is sauce for it. *Striking Him Again* You call'd me yesterday mountain-squire; but I will make you to-day a squire of low degree. I pray you fall to; if you can mock a leek, you can eat a leek.

GOWER: Enough, Captain, you have astonish'd him.

FLUELLEN: I say I will make him eat some part of my leek, or I will peat his pate four days. Bite, I pray you, it is good for your green wound and your ploody coxcomb.

PISTOL: Must I bite?

FLUELLEN: Yes, certainly, and out of doubt, and out of question too, and ambiguides.

PISTOL: By this leek, I will most horribly revenge- I eat and eat, I swear-

FLUELLEN: Eat, I pray you; will you have some more sauce to your leek? There is not enough leek to swear by.

PISTOL: Quiet thy cudgel: thou dost see I eat.

FLUELLEN: Much good do you, scald knave, heartily. Nay, pray you throw none away; the skin is good for your broken coxcomb. When you take occasions to see leeks hereafter, I pray you mock at 'em; that is all.

PISTOL: Good.

FLUELLEN: Ay, leeks is good. Hold you, there is a groat to heal your pate.

PISTOL: Me a groat!

FLUELLEN: Yes, verily and in truth, you shall take it; or I have another leek in my pocket which you shall eat.

PISTOL: I take thy groat in earnest of revenge.

FLUELLEN: If I owe you anything I will pay you in cudgels; you shall be a woodmonger, and buy nothing of me but cudgels. God bye you, and keep you, and heal your pate.
Exit

PISTOL: All hell shall stir for this.

GOWER: Go, go: you are a couterfeit cowardly knave. Will you mock at an ancient tradition, begun upon an honourable respect, and worn as a memorable trophy of predeceased valour, and dare not avouch in your deeds any of your words? I have seen you gleeking and galling at this gentleman twice or thrice. You thought, because he could not speak English in the native garb, he could not therefore handle an English cudgel; you find it otherwise, and henceforth let a Welsh correction teach you a good English condition. Fare ye well.
Exit

PISTOL: Doth Fortune play the huswife with me now?
News have I that my Nell is dead i' th' spital
Of malady of France;
And there my rendezvous is quite cut off.
Old I do wax; and from my weary limbs

Honour is cudgell'd. Well, bawd I'll turn,
And something lean to cutpurse of quick hand.
To England will I steal, and there I'll steal;
And patches will I get unto these cudgell'd scars,
And swear I got them in the Gallia wars.
Exit

ACT V. SCENE II. France. The French King's Palace

Enter at One Door, King Henry, Exeter, Bedford, Gloucester, Warwick, Westmoreland, and Other Lords; at Another, the French King, Queen Isabel, the Princess Katherine, Alice, and Other Ladies; the Duke of Burgundy, and His Train

KING HENRY: Peace to this meeting, wherefore we are met!
Unto our brother France, and to our sister,
Health and fair time of day; joy and good wishes
To our most fair and princely cousin Katherine.
And, as a branch and member of this royalty,
By whom this great assembly is contriv'd,
We do salute you, Duke of Burgundy.
And, princes French, and peers, health to you all!

FRENCH KING: Right joyous are we to behold your face,
Most worthy brother England; fairly met!
So are you, princes English, every one.

QUEEN ISABEL: So happy be the issue, brother England,
Of this good day and of this gracious meeting
As we are now glad to behold your eyes-
Your eyes, which hitherto have home in them,
Against the French that met them in their bent,
The fatal balls of murdering basilisks;
The venom of such looks, we fairly hope,
Have lost their quality; and that this day
Shall change all griefs and quarrels into love.

KING HENRY: To cry amen to that, thus we appear.

QUEEN ISABEL: You English princes an, I do salute you.

BURGUNDY: My duty to you both, on equal love,
Great Kings of France and England! That I have labour'd
With all my wits, my pains, and strong endeavours,
To bring your most imperial Majesties
Unto this bar and royal interview,
Your mightiness on both parts best can witness.
Since then my office hath so far prevail'd
That face to face and royal eye to eye
You have congreeted, let it not disgrace me
If I demand, before this royal view,
What rub or what impediment there is
Why that the naked, poor, and mangled Peace,
Dear nurse of arts, plenties, and joyful births,
Should not in this best garden of the world,
Our fertile France, put up her lovely visage?
Alas, she hath from France too long been chas'd!
And all her husbandry doth lie on heaps,
Corrupting in it own fertility.
Her vine, the merry cheerer of the heart,
Unpruned dies; her hedges even-pleach'd,
Like prisoners wildly overgrown with hair,
Put forth disorder'd twigs; her fallow leas
The darnel, hemlock, and rank fumitory,
Doth root upon, while that the coulter rusts
That should deracinate such savagery;
The even mead, that erst brought sweetly forth
The freckled cowslip, burnet, and green clover,
Wanting the scythe, all uncorrected, rank,
Conceives by idleness, and nothing teems
But hateful docks, rough thistles, kecksies, burs,
Losing both beauty and utility.
And as our vineyards, fallows, meads, and hedges,
Defective in their natures, grow to wildness;
Even so our houses and ourselves and children
Have lost, or do not learn for want of time,

The sciences that should become our country;
But grow, like savages- as soldiers will,
That nothing do but meditate on blood-
To swearing and stern looks, diffus'd attire,
And everything that seems unnatural.
Which to reduce into our former favout
You are assembled; and my speech entreats
That I may know the let why gentle Peace
Should not expel these inconveniences
And bless us with her former qualities.

KING HENRY: If, Duke of Burgundy, you would the peace
Whose want gives growth to th' imperfections
Which you have cited, you must buy that peace
With full accord to all our just demands;
Whose tenours and particular effects
You have, enschedul'd briefly, in your hands.

BURGUNDY: The King hath heard them; to the which as yet
There is no answer made.

KING HENRY: Well then, the peace,
Which you before so urg'd, lies in his answer.

FRENCH KING: I have but with a cursorary eye
O'erglanced the articles; pleaseth your Grace
To appoint some of your council presently
To sit with us once more, with better heed
To re-survey them, we will suddenly
Pass our accept and peremptory answer.

KING HENRY: Brother, we shall. Go, uncle Exeter,
And brother Clarence, and you, brother Gloucester,
Warwick, and Huntington, go with the King;
And take with you free power to ratify,
Augment, or alter, as your wisdoms best
Shall see advantageable for our dignity,

Any thing in or out of our demands;
And we'll consign thereto. Will you, fair sister,
Go with the princes or stay here with us?

QUEEN ISABEL: Our gracious brother, I will go with them;
Haply a woman's voice may do some good,
When articles too nicely urg'd be stood on.

KING HENRY: Yet leave our cousin Katherine here with us;
She is our capital demand, compris'd
Within the fore-rank of our articles.

QUEEN ISABEL: She hath good leave.
Exeunt All but the King, Katherine, and Alice

KING HENRY: Fair Katherine, and most fair,
Will you vouchsafe to teach a soldier terms
Such as will enter at a lady's ear,
And plead his love-suit to her gentle heart?

KATHERINE: Your Majesty shall mock me; I cannot speak your England.

KING HENRY: O fair Katherine, if you will love me soundly with your French heart, I will be glad to hear you confess it brokenly with your English tongue. Do you like me, Kate?

KATHERINE: Pardonnez-moi, I cannot tell vat is like me.

KING HENRY: An angel is like you, Kate, and you are like an angel.

KATHERINE: Que dit-il? que je suis semblable a les anges?

ALICE: Oui, vraiment, sauf votre grace, ainsi dit-il.

KING HENRY: I said so, dear Katherine, and I must not blush to affirm it.

KATHERINE: O bon Dieu! les langues des hommes sont pleines de tromperies.

KING HENRY: What says she, fair one? that the tongues of men are full of deceits?

ALICE: Oui, dat de tongues of de mans is be full of deceits- dat is de Princess.

KING HENRY: The Princess is the better English-woman. I' faith, Kate, my wooing is fit for thy understanding: I am glad thou canst speak no better English; for if thou couldst, thou wouldst find me such a plain king that thou wouldst think I had sold my farm to buy my crown. I know no ways to mince it in love, but directly to say 'I love you.' Then, if you urge me farther than to say 'Do you in faith?' I wear out my suit. Give me your answer; i' faith, do; and so clap hands and a bargain. How say you, lady?

KATHERINE: Sauf votre honneur, me understand well.

KING HENRY: Marry, if you would put me to verses or to dance for your sake, Kate, why you undid me; for the one I have neither words nor measure, and for the other I have no strength in measure, yet a reasonable measure in strength. If I could win a lady at leap-frog, or by vaulting into my saddle with my armour on my back, under the correction of bragging be it spoken, I should quickly leap into wife. Or if I might buffet for my love, or bound my horse for her favours, I could lay on like a butcher, and sit like a jack-an-apes, never off. But, before God, Kate, I cannot look greenly, nor gasp out my cloquence, nor I have no cunning in protestation; only downright oaths, which I never use till urg'd, nor never break for urging. If thou canst love a fellow of this temper, Kate, whose face is not worth sunburning, that never looks in his glass for love of anything he sees there, let thine eye be thy cook. I speak to thee plain soldier. If thou canst love me for this, take me; if not, to say to thee that I shall die is true- but for thy love, by the Lord, no; yet I love thee too. And while thou liv'st, dear Kate, take a fellow of plain and uncoined constancy; for he perforce must do thee right, because he hath not the gift to woo in other places; for these fellows of infinite tongue, that can rhyme themselves into ladies' favours, they do always reason themselves out again. What! a speaker is but a prater: a rhyme is but a ballad. A good leg will fall; a straight back will stoop; a black beard will turn white; a curl'd pate will grow bald; a fair face will wither; a full eye will wax hollow. But a good heart, Kate, is the sun and the moon; or, rather, the sun, and not the moon- for it shines bright and never changes, but keeps his course truly. If thou would have such a one, take me; and take me, take a soldier; take a soldier, take a king. And what say'st thou, then, to my love? Speak, my fair, and fairly, I pray thee.

KATHERINE: Is it possible dat I sould love de enemy of France?

KING HENRY: No, it is not possible you should love the enemy of France, Kate, but in loving me you should love the friend of France; for I love France so well that I will not part with a village of it; I will have it all mine. And, Kate, when France is mine and I am yours, then yours is France and you are mine.

KATHERINE: I cannot tell vat is dat.

KING HENRY: No, Kate? I will tell thee in French, which I am sure will hang upon my tongue like a new-married wife about her husband's neck, hardly to be shook off. Je quand sur le possession de France, et quand vous avez le possession de moi- let me see, what then? Saint Denis be my speed!- donc votre est France et vous etes mienne. It is as easy for me, Kate, to conquer the kingdom as to speak so much more French: I shall never move thee in French, unless it be to laugh at me.

KATHERINE: Sauf votre honneur, le Francais que vous parlez, il est meilleur que l'Anglais lequel je parle.

KING HENRY: No, faith, is't not, Kate; but thy speaking of my tongue, and I thine, most truly falsely, must needs be granted to be much at one. But, Kate, dost thou understand thus much English- Canst thou love me?

KATHERINE: I cannot tell.

KING HENRY: Can any of your neighbours tell, Kate? I'll ask them. Come, I know thou lovest me; and at night, when you come into your closet, you'll question this gentlewoman about me; and I know, Kate, you will to her dispraise those parts in me that you love with your heart. But, good Kate, mock me mercifully; the rather, gentle Princess, because I love thee cruelly. If ever thou beest mine, Kate, as I have a saving faith within me tells me thou shalt, I get thee with scambling, and thou must therefore needs prove a good soldier-breeder. Shall not thou and I, between Saint Denis and Saint George, compound a boy, half French, half English, that shall go to Constantinople and take the Turk by the beard? Shall we not? What say'st thou, my fair flower-de-luce?

KATHERINE: I do not know dat.

KING HENRY: No: 'tis hereafter to know, but now to promise; do but now promise, Kate, you will endeavour for your French part of such a boy; and for my English moiety take the word of a king and a bachelor. How answer you, la plus belle Katherine du monde, mon tres cher et divin deesse?

KATHERINE: Your Majestee ave fausse French enough to deceive de most sage damoiselle dat is en France.

KING HENRY: Now, fie upon my false French! By mine honour, in true English, I love thee, Kate; by which honour I dare not swear thou lovest me; yet my blood begins to flatter me that thou dost, notwithstanding the poor and untempering effect of my visage. Now beshrew my father's ambition! He was thinking of civil wars when he got me; therefore was I created with a stubborn outside, with an aspect of iron, that when I come to woo ladies I fright them. But, in faith, Kate, the elder I wax, the better I shall appear: my comfort is, that old age, that in layer-up of beauty, can do no more spoil upon my face; thou hast me, if thou hast me, at the worst; and thou shalt wear me, if thou wear me, better and better. And therefore tell me, most fair Katherine, will you have me? Put off your maiden blushes; avouch the thoughts of your heart with the looks of an empress; take me by the hand and say 'Harry of England, I am thine.' Which word thou shalt no sooner bless mine ear withal but I will tell thee aloud 'England is thine, Ireland is thine, France is thine, and Henry Plantagenet is thine'; who, though I speak it before his face, if he be not fellow with the best king, thou shalt find the best king of good fellows. Come, your answer in broken music- for thy voice is music and thy English broken; therefore, Queen of all, Katherine, break thy mind to me in broken English, wilt thou have me?

KATHERINE: Dat is as it shall please de roi mon pere.

KING HENRY: Nay, it will please him well, Kate- it shall please him, Kate.

KATHERINE: Den it sall also content me.

KING HENRY: Upon that I kiss your hand, and I can you my queen.

KATHERINE: Laissez, mon seigneur, laissez, laissez! Ma foi, je ne veux point que vous abaissiez votre grandeur en baisant la main d'une, notre seigneur, indigne serviteur; excusez-moi, je vous supplie, mon tres puissant seigneur.

KING HENRY: Then I will kiss your lips, Kate.

KATHERINE: Les dames et demoiselles pour etre baisees devant leur noces, il n'est pas la coutume de France.

KING HENRY: Madame my interpreter, what says she?

ALICE: Dat it is not be de fashion pour le ladies of France- I cannot tell vat is baiser en Anglish.

KING HENRY: To kiss.

ALICE: Your Majestee entendre bettre que moi.

KING HENRY: It is not a fashion for the maids in France to kiss before they are married, would she say?

ALICE: Oui, vraiment.

KING HENRY: O Kate, nice customs curtsy to great kings. Dear Kate, you and I cannot be confin'd within the weak list of a country's fashion; we are the makers of manners, Kate; and the liberty that follows our places stops the mouth of all find-faults- as I will do yours for upholding the nice fashion of your country in denying me a kiss; therefore, patiently and yielding. *Kissing Her* You have witchcraft in your lips, Kate: there is more eloquence in a sugar touch of them than in the tongues of the French council; and they should sooner persuade Henry of England than a general petition of monarchs. Here comes your father.

Enter the French Power and the English Lords

BURGUNDY: God save your Majesty! My royal cousin,
Teach you our princess English?

KING HENRY: I would have her learn, my fair cousin, how perfectly I love her; and that is good English.

BURGUNDY: Is she not apt?

KING HENRY: Our tongue is rough, coz, and my condition is not smooth; so that, having neither the voice nor the heart of flattery about me, I cannot so conjure up the spirit of love in her that he will appear in his true likeness.

BURGUNDY: Pardon the frankness of my mirth, if I answer you for that. If you would conjure in her, you must make a circle; if conjure up love in her in his true likeness, he must appear naked and blind. Can you blame her, then, being a maid yet ros'd over with the virgin crimson of modesty, if she deny the appearance of a naked blind boy in her naked seeing self? It were, my lord, a hard condition for a maid to consign to.

KING HENRY: Yet they do wink and yield, as love is blind and enforces.

BURGUNDY: They are then excus'd, my lord, when they see not what they do.

KING HENRY: Then, good my lord, teach your cousin to consent winking.

BURGUNDY: I will wink on her to consent, my lord, if you will teach her to know my meaning; for maids well summer'd and warm kept are like flies at Bartholomew-tide, blind, though they have their eyes; and then they will endure handling, which before would not abide looking on.

KING HENRY: This moral ties me over to time and a hot summer; and so I shall catch the fly, your cousin, in the latter end, and she must be blind too.

BURGUNDY: As love is, my lord, before it loves.

KING HENRY: It is so; and you may, some of you, thank love for my blindness, who cannot see many a fair French city for one fair French maid that stands in my way.

FRENCH KING: Yes, my lord, you see them perspectively, the cities turned into a maid; for they are all girdled with maiden walls that war hath never ent'red.

KING HENRY: Shall Kate be my wife?

FRENCH KING: So please you.

KING HENRY: I am content, so the maiden cities you talk of may wait on her; so the maid that stood in the way for my wish shall show me the way to my will.

FRENCH KING: We have consented to all terms of reason.

KING HENRY: Is't so, my lords of England?

WESTMORELAND: The king hath granted every article:
His daughter first; and then in sequel, all,
According to their firm proposed natures.

EXETER: Only he hath not yet subscribed this: Where your Majesty demands that the King of France, having any occasion to write for matter of grant, shall name your Highness in this form and with this addition, in

French, Notre tres cher fils Henri, Roi d'Angleterre, Heritier de France; and thus in Latin, Praeclarissimus filius noster Henricus, Rex Angliae et Haeres Franciae.

FRENCH KING: Nor this I have not, brother, so denied But our request shall make me let it pass.

KING HENRY: I pray you, then, in love and dear alliance,
Let that one article rank with the rest;
And thereupon give me your daughter.

FRENCH KING: Take her, fair son, and from her blood raise up
Issue to me; that the contending kingdoms
Of France and England, whose very shores look pale
With envy of each other's happiness,
May cease their hatred; and this dear conjunction
Plant neighbourhood and Christian-like accord
In their sweet bosoms, that never war advance
His bleeding sword 'twixt England and fair France.

LORDS: Amen!

KING HENRY: Now, welcome, Kate; and bear me witness all,
That here I kiss her as my sovereign queen. *Floulish*

QUEEN ISABEL: God, the best maker of all marriages,
Combine your hearts in one, your realms in one!
As man and wife, being two, are one in love,
So be there 'twixt your kingdoms such a spousal
That never may ill office or fell jealousy,
Which troubles oft the bed of blessed marriage,
Thrust in between the paction of these kingdoms,
To make divorce of their incorporate league;
That English may as French, French Englishmen,
Receive each other. God speak this Amen!

ALL: Amen!

KING HENRY: Prepare we for our marriage; on which day,
My Lord of Burgundy, we'll take your oath,
And all the peers', for surety of our leagues.
Then shall I swear to Kate, and you to me,
And may our oaths well kept and prosp'rous be!
Sennet. Exeunt

EPILOGUE.

Enter Chorus

CHORUS: Thus far, with rough and all-unable pen,
Our bending author hath pursu'd the story,
In little room confining mighty men,
Mangling by starts the full course of their glory.
Small time, but, in that small, most greatly lived
This star of England. Fortune made his sword;
By which the world's best garden he achieved,
And of it left his son imperial lord.
Henry the Sixth, in infant bands crown'd king
Of France and England, did this king succeed;
Whose state so many had the managing
That they lost France and made his England bleed;
Which oft our stage hath shown; and, for their sake,
In your fair minds let this acceptance take.
Exit

END

www.ingramcontent.com/pod-product-compliance
Lightning Source LLC
LaVergne TN
LVHW090615110826
845146LV00001B/401

* 9 7 9 8 8 8 0 9 1 7 4 0 2 *